HEIDEGGER AND THE GROUND OF ETHICS

Existential philosophy has often been identified with moral nihilism and the idea that everything is permitted. This book shows that, in the case of Martin Heidegger, any such assumption seriously distorts the true character of his thought. In *Being and Time* Heidegger sketches a concept of human co-existence as *Mitsein* – our being together with one another in the world. He also makes clear that *Mitsein* has ethical implications, although he failed to develop them in any detail. This study carries forward the analysis of the ethical character of *Mitsein* and at several points moves significantly beyond Heidegger's account of it.

Written by one of the preeminent interpreters of Heidegger, this book is an important statement about the basis of human sociality. It is a major contribution to the continuing debates about Heidegger in particular and ethics in general.

MODERN EUROPEAN PHILOSOPHY

This series contains a range of high-quality books on philosophers, topics, and schools of thought prominent in the Kantian and post-Kantian European tradition. It is nonsectarian in approach and methodology, and includes both introductory and more specialized treatments of these thinkers and topics. Authors are encouraged to interpret the boundaries of the modern European tradition in a broad way and in primarily philosophical rather than historical terms.

General Editor
ROBERT B. PIPPIN, University of Chicago

Advisory Board
GARY GUTTING, University of Notre Dame
ROLF-PETER HORSTMANN, Humboldt University, Berlin
MARK SACKS, University of Essex

Some Recent Titles:
Frederick A. Olafson: *What Is a Human Being?*
Stanley Rosen: *The Mask of Enlightenment: Nietzsche's Zarathustra*
Robert C. Scharff: *Comte After Positivism*
F. C. T. Moore: *Bergson: Thinking Backwards*
Charles Larmore: *The Morals of Modernity*
Robert B. Pippin: *Idealism as Modernism*
Daniel W. Conway: *Nietzsche's Dangerous Game*
John P. McCormick: *Carl Schmitt's Critique of Liberalism*
Günter Zöller: *Fichte's Transcendental Philosophy*

HEIDEGGER AND THE
GROUND OF ETHICS

A STUDY OF *MITSEIN*

FREDERICK A. OLAFSON

CAMBRIDGE
UNIVERSITY PRESS

PUBLISHED BY THE PRESS SYNDICATE OF THE UNIVERSITY OF CAMBRIDGE
The Pitt Building, Trumpington Street, Cambridge CB2 1RP, United Kingdom

CAMBRIDGE UNIVERSITY PRESS
The Edinburgh Building, Cambridge CB2 2RU, UK   http://www.cup.cam.ac.uk
40 West 20th Street, New York, NY 10011-4211, USA   http://www.cup.org
10 Stamford Road, Oakleigh, Melbourne 3166, Australia

© Frederick A. Olafson 1998

First published 1998

Printed in the United States of America

Typeset in Baskerville 10.25/13 pt, in Quark XPress™ [AG]

*A catalog record for this book is available from
the British Library*

Library of Congress Cataloging-in-Publication Data
Olafson, Frederick A.
Heidegger and the ground of ethics : a study of Mitsein / Frederick
A. Olafson.
p.   cm. – (Modern European philosophy)
ISBN 0-521-63094-0 ISBN 0-521-63879-8 (pbk)
1. Heidegger, Martin, 1889–1976 – Ethics.   2. Ethics, Modern – 20th
century.   I. Title.   II. Series.
B3279.H490368   1998
171'.2 – dc21   98–16539
                                                                CIP

ISBN 0 521 63094 0 hardback
ISBN 0 521 63879 8 paperback

FOR
SAM AND ANNE KING
IN FRIENDSHIP

CONTENTS

INTRODUCTION

Das unter dem Anspruch der Anwesenheit Stehen is der grösste Anspruch des Menschen, ist "die Ethik."[1]

Martin Heidegger

I

When existential philosophy first became widely known in the years after the Second World War, it was understood to be a radically individualistic philosophy. It is not hard to see why this was so. For these philosophers, every aspect of human life was to be understood in terms of the concept of choice; and choice was held to be in every case the choice of an individual human being, however we might try to conceal this fact from ourselves. Such choices were declared to be ultimately arbitrary and unjustifiable by the procedures of reason. If there was any virtue that survived the wreck of all traditional conceptions of moral truth and validity, it was the ability to accept this grim fact and live "authentically" with it. This meant living in a way that did not invoke any authority for one's own actions that was inconsistent with these underlying assumptions.[2]

---

1 "To be subject to the claim that presence makes is the greatest claim that a human being makes; it is what 'ethics' is." Martin Heidegger, *Zollikoner Seminare* (Frankfurt am Main: V. Klostermann, 1987), p. 273. These seminars were given in Switzerland late in Heidegger's life. It is worth noting that this quotation expresses both the strength and the weakness of Heidegger's way of locating "ethics." It explicitly connects presence (*Anwesenheit*) with ethics, but it does not acknowledge the even more important connection of ethics with *reciprocal* presence and thus with *Mitsein*. The trouble with this association of presence (but not reciprocal presence) with ethics is that it issues in a conception of the relation of thought to the truth of being as "the original ethic" without any reference to our relation to one another. See the relevant quotations on this subject in note 5.

In some ways, an even better quotation to set at the beginning of a work like this would be what Saint Paul says in Ephesians 4:25: "Therefore speak the truth for we are the members one of another." Interestingly, the Greek word for truth that Saint Paul uses is *aletheia*, which figures prominently in Heidegger's own thought.

2 My interest in these themes is of long standing and goes back to an early book of mine, *Principles and Persons: An Ethical Interpretation of Existentialism* (Baltimore: Johns Hopkins University Press, 1967). In that book I tried, among other things, to show that there was a linkage between the concept of authenticity, which has played such an important role in existential philosophy, and that of moral obligation, which has hardly figured there at all.

In the version of these ideas that we owe to Jean-Paul Sartre, this individualistic theme was taken as far as it could logically go. The same holds true
for any implications it might be supposed to have for the ethical character
of our relations with other human beings. According to Sartre, these relations could only be one form or another of domination; as he put it, they
would unavoidably be either sadistic or masochistic. No true mutuality was
possible; and even the Kantian attempt to conceive and treat other human
beings as ends in themselves was declared to be a unilateral exercise of
power over them.[3] In other formulations after the end of the war, Sartre soft-
ened these harsh implications of his ontology of freedom, doubtless because
they were hard to reconcile with his social and political activism at that time.
There is no evidence, however, that he ever modified them until the very
end of his philosophical career, when he threw out some ideas of a quite different kind that have a special importance for the purposes of this study.
These will be brought into this discussion at a later point.[4]

That suggestion certainly had an air of paradox about it; and it was not well received by those
who commented on the book. Nevertheless, I am still convinced that it has merit. What I
have come to see, however, in the course of subsequent work largely concerned with different aspects of Heidegger's thought, is that what was missing in the account I gave in that early
work was a fuller ontological concept of human nature itself. I have worked out such an account in two more recent studies, *Heidegger and the Philosophy of Mind* (New Haven: Yale University Press, 1987) and *What Is a Human Being?: A Heideggerian View* (Cambridge University
Press, 1995). In the Conclusion to the latter book, I pointed out that the fact of the plurality or "manyness" of human beings had not been brought – explicitly – into the ontological
analysis I had given of human nature, although it was presupposed in it. I also suggested that
the key to an understanding of how this could be done lay in Heidegger's conception of what
we usually call "intersubjectivity" as "being with one another" (*Miteinandersein* or, more commonly, *Mitsein*). My thought was that if that conception could be developed beyond the very
brief sketch he gave of it in *Being and Time*, it might be possible to show that it has at least a
proto-ethical character and that this would be of fundamental importance for any inquiry
into the ground of ethics. That is the task I am undertaking here. In some sense, then, this
study is an amplification of both the line of thought I was trying to develop thirty years ago
and of the powerfully suggestive but all-too-brief account Heidegger gave of *Mitsein* in *Being
and Time.*

3 In a popular exposition of his views that Sartre presented as a lecture in 1946 and that was
subsequently published as *Existentialism and Humanism*, translated by P. Mairet (London:
Methuen, 1948), he takes a very Kantian line and argues that I cannot consistently desire my
own freedom without desiring that of others. That kind of logical consistency would have
meant nothing to the author of *Being and Nothingness* (translated by Hazel Barnes [New York:
Philosophical Library, 1956]); and it cannot have meant much to him even in 1946 since he
took no notice of the flagrant conflict between this thesis and the line of thought developed
in his earlier work.

4 A year or two before the 1946 lecture, Sartre wrote his play *No Exit*, containing the famous
line, "Hell is other people" – not exactly a Kantian sentiment, but one quite consistent with
the theses of *Being and Nothingness*. Even so, at the end of that work, Sartre promised a book
on ethics that would explore the possibility that the kind of freedom that he celebrated in
Being and Nothingness could itself become the basis for an ethic. The conception of ethics that

The general theory of human being from which these drastic conclusions were drawn was strongly influenced by the thought of Martin Heidegger, which had been developed in the aftermath of the First World War, as Sartre's was during the Second. Heidegger repudiated any suggestion of an affinity between his thought and that of Sartre; and there can be no doubt that in matters of ontology Sartre departed quite significantly from the line of thought of his predecessor. Even so, there is much in *Being and Nothingness* that echoes themes in *Being and Time*. In both, a concept of radical choice was made the basis of an authentic human life and the concept of authenticity as a kind of existential ideal that had been elaborated by Heidegger was taken over by Sartre. More generally, although Heidegger never dealt directly with questions of normative ethics, there was, in *Being and Time*, a very harsh critique of the whole conception of "values" as objective criteria for the guidance of our lives. These were declared to belong to an anonymous public mode of selfhood – what Heidegger called *das Man* – the "One," as in "One says . . ." – that occludes both the individuality and the distinctive ontological character of human being. At bottom, it is a set of defenses by which we human beings hide our freedom from ourselves. But it was possible, Heidegger claimed, to dismantle these defenses, at least partly, and to emerge into a new kind of responsibility for one's own life. Whether the state of being into which one would so emerge could have an ethical character that would be consistent with this new freedom was a question Heidegger did not pose in this form and certainly did not answer.

But even if the world contains no moral signposts, there is still the question of whether our relation to one another can by itself yield standards of right and wrong. The concept of authenticity is pretty clearly one that most readily applies to the situation of individual human beings. But if the illusionless freedom it represents is to have any meaning in a life that we share with other people, it would have to be made clear how we can be authentic together. Heidegger never did that, but there is in *Being and Time* a section devoted to what he calls *Mitsein* – our being in the world together with one another. It is not just an empirical fact, he argues, that there are many human beings in the world. Our being *with* other like entities is, instead, a

Sartre had in mind was evidently still completely individualistic in character; and there was no suggestion that any bond between human beings that would constitute them as a "We," not to speak of any concept of obligation, was in prospect. In any case, that promised book never appeared; and when the notebooks that contained Sartre's preparatory studies for it were posthumously published as *Cahiers pour une morale* (Paris: Gallimard, 1983), there was nothing to indicate that Sartre's conception of ethics had been broadened in any significant way. It appears that, instead, he was engaged in developing the new line of thought that came to expression in his *Critique de la raison dialectique* (1960), in which a kind of Marxism was grafted onto an existentialist base. It was only in an interview given a year or two before his death that Sartre rejected the theses of both *Being and Nothingness* and *Critique of Dialectical Reason* and proposed the idea of an ontologically based ethic of the "We."

constitutive element in our own mode of being as it is in theirs; and it is one to which we cannot do justice as long as we approach it via traditional philosophical routes like the theory of empathy. What is even more interesting is the fact that in characterizing our *Mitsein* Heidegger invokes at least one other concept to which an unmistakably ethical character attachs. This is the concept of *Fürsorge* – one human being's caring about another – and it is this caring that he declares to be, in its several modalities, central to our being with one another. On the strength of these theses, he is even willing to go so far as to state that we are, as he puts it, "for the sake of others" (*umwillen Anderer*). Because this idea was never developed further and Heidegger's occasional reflections on ethics in his later period take a quite different line, we have no explanation of how the concept of *Mitsein* generates the notion of *Fürsorge*.[5] Significantly, however, he claims that "resoluteness" – an exis-

5 For Heidegger's later view of ethics, see his "Brief uber den Humanismus," in *Wegmarken* (Frankfurt am Main: V. Kostermann, 1967), pp. 145–94. This essay has greatly influenced, in a negative sense, the interpretation of Heidegger's attitude toward an interest in humanity and in ethics, especially in France but elsewhere as well. The unfortunate result of this approach has been that his later writings – from the mid-1930s onward – have controlled the interpretation of his thought as a whole and the strong interest shown in *Being and Time* in a specifically human mode of being has been more or less dismissed. In this way Heidegger became a kind of patron saint for all the intellectual tendencies that have been trying for several decades to put the human subject out of business. (On this topic, see Luc Ferry and Michel Renaut, *La pensée 68*: Essai sur l'anti-humanisme contemporain [Paris: Gallimard, 1985].) Admittedly, Heidegger's own statements on this subject are hardly consistent, but it is difficult to see him as unqualifiedly repudiating the concept of a subject. After all, *Dasein* was described in *Being and Time* as a subject-entity (*seiendes Subjekt*); and in the late *Zollikoner Seminare* Heidegger invoked the concept of *Dasein* and showed the same interest in the kind of entity a human being is as he did at the time of *Being and Time*. He also said, as few antihumanists would, that humanism had in some sense underestimated the dignity of man by failing to do justice to his relation to being.

Even so, the "Letter on Humanism" marks a high point in Heidegger's campaign against traditional humanism; and one of the main targets is once again the concept of values. This time, though, the grounds of his opposition appear to have widened considerably. In *Being and Time*, the trouble with values was that they were creatures of *Das Man* and, as supposedly preexistent attributes of things or situations, relieved people of the necessity to choose. In the later essay, choice is not mentioned at all; and Heidegger's argument against values is that they involve an unacceptable subjectivization of being. "All evaluation (*Werten*) is a subjectivization, even when it evaluates something positively. It does not let entities *be;* evaluation grants them validity (*lässt gelten*) only as the object of its own action" ("Brief über den Humanismus," p. 179). In what sense evaluations would be "subjective" is left unexplained: but it looks very much as though any action by a human being that rests on a judgment that one outcome is preferable to another would be subjective in this undefined but clearly negative sense. But then if "letting entities be" is the only way to avoid subjectivism, we would have to give up the active life altogether and adopt a wholly passive stance as satellites of being. If this were accepted, it would seem to obviate the need for anything like an ethic; but Heidegger also wants to claim that the kind of "thought that thinks the truth of being as the initial (*anfänglich*) element in a human being as an ek-sistent is in itself the original ethic" (p. 187). For all his hatred of preestablished formulas for the guidance of conduct, he is

tential virtue closely akin to authenticity – "pushes us into a caring *Mitsein* with others."[6]

It is these texts of Heidegger's that will provide the point of departure for this study. There is, however, at least one other philosopher who was notable for his willingness to conceive *Mitsein* – what he called *être pour autrui* – in positive terms. Maurice Merleau-Ponty was an existential phenomenologist whose thought drew on many of the same sources as did that of Heidegger and Sartre and, while highly distinctive in its own right, stands in a close relation of affiliation with theirs.[7] Unlike Sartre, who denied that it could have any ethical character, Merleau-Ponty invariably made the sociality of human existence central to a wide range of human functions; he carried on a life-long debate with Sartre on this topic. Although he did not, in his all-too-brief philosophical career, ever develop a theory of *Mitsein* as an ethical condition, it is not far-fetched to surmise that his influence must have counted for something in the extraordinary turnabout that Sartre effected at the end of his life. Sartre was not a man who had ever felt constrained by any requirement of fidelity to the positions he had previously held. Nevertheless, it was quite astonishing that he should repudiate, as he did in an interview given in 1978, the whole doctrine set forth in *Being and Nothingness* and speak, cryptically but intriguingly, of a distinctive *relation humaine* and an ontologically based ethic of the "We."[8]

This last phrase expresses very well the intention of this study, which will draw on the work of all these philosophers in order to work out a concept

even willing to go so far as to say that "only insofar as man, ek-sisting in the truth of being, belongs to being, can the directions (*Weisungen*) come from being that must be law and rule for man" (p. 191). This makes it sound as though any normative contrast asserted by a human being must offend against the dignity of being since it presumes to set itself up in some degree of independence from the being that is now described as the source of the "rules" by which we are to live. Being, in other words, is not just a necessary condition for an ethic but apparently a sufficient condition as well. This has a familiar – indeed, a quite traditional – ring to it, but it can hardly be reconciled with the theses of *Being and Time*. Somehow, it does not come as a surprise that this conception of ethics gives no account at all of our relations to other human beings – that is, our being with one another.

For a discussion of the relationship between ethics and ontology in Heidegger's thought, see Joanna Hodge, *Heidegger and Ethics* (Routledge: London, 1995). Unfortunately, there is no analysis of *Mitsein* in this book and no suggestion that it might have any ethical implications.

6 The discussion of *Mitsein* and *Fürsorge* comes in ch. 4 of Division 1 of Part I in *Being and Time*, translated by J. Macquarrie and E. Robinson (New York: Harper and Row, 1962). The passage about resoluteness and *Fürsorge* is on p. 344 of *Being and Time* (p. 298 in the German edition: *Sein und Zeit* [Tübingen: Max Niemeyer Verlag, 1957]).

7 The best exposition of Merleau-Ponty's views on being with others can be found in his *Phenomenology of Perception*, translated by Colin Smith (London: Routledge and Kegan Paul, 1962), Part II, ch. 4, "Other Selves and the Human World."

8 "J.-P. Sartre et M. Sicard: Entretien," *Obliques* (Paris: Editions Borderie, 1978), nos. 18–19, pp. 9–29.

of *Mitsein* as the ground of ethics. It will, however, be Heidegger's account of *Mitsein* that will serve as the main exegetical basis for the line of thought I want to develop. Since at the same time as I build on his account of *Mitsein* I will also be trying to amplify it quite significantly, a certain tension in my relation to his thought may result that could prove rather confusing. The complexity here is due to the fact that I am engaged in a dual undertaking: extracting a key idea from the work of another philosopher and trying to develop it independently. (By way of justification, it could be said that Heidegger did very much the same thing in his interpretation of Kant's doctrine of the schematism, which he took out of its context in the *Critique of Pure Reason* and greatly amplified so as to make of it his own concept of temporality.)

My primary concern in all this is not to vindicate Heidegger, the man, against his many critics. It is rather to show that the profoundly original constellation of ideas he introduced in *Being and Time* can make an important contribution to our understanding of the whole ethical side of our lives. I am deeply convinced that those ideas need not lead to nihilism, as they have been almost universally supposed to do; and I want to show that there is a quite different way in which the ethical implications of existential philosophy can be construed. What I am trying to do is to show that there is a fundamental insight in Heidegger's account of *Mitsein* that he did not develop, although he appears to have had a sense of its ethical significance. By way of proof that this insight is not just an invention of mine, I rely chiefly on the fact that, in the matter of *Fürsorge* on which I have already touched, Heidegger himself asserts a strong linkage between it and our being with one another. There is plainly a large hermeneutical question here as to why a philosopher who had achieved the kind of insight into the character of the relations of human beings to one another that I impute to Heidegger never developed it beyond the brief formulation offered to us in *Being and Time*. I do not try to answer that question, both because I am not sure I can and because to do so would take me too far from my real theme: the ethical potentialities of the concept of *Mitsein*. But all these matters are finally of secondary importance because, for all my great debt to Heidegger's thought, what I am proposing is a constructive philosophical account of the ground of ethics, and this must be judged on its own merits.

This book does not claim to be an exhaustive treatment of its subject. What I offer here are "essays" in the original sense of that word. As such, they have many lacunae and they do not attempt to anticipate every criticism that might be made of the theses being proposed. What they do attempt is to set forth what I take to be the central elements of any theory that would build on the concept of *Mitsein*. In this spirit, then, I begin in Chapter 1 with an account of the special character of the being-with-one-another of human beings; and although the account I give is, I believe, faithful to Heidegger's thought, it also attempts a kind of reconstruction of his conception of *Mitsein* with a view to a formulation of its ethical import. Then, in Chapter 2, the concept of caring about others as a fundamental element in *Mitsein* is taken up. Heidegger's treatment of this concept is examined; and I try to show that it does not enable us to understand the linkage between our being-with-one-another and our caring about one another (*Fürsorge*), although this is something to which Heidegger was explicitly committed. More specifically, it cannot generate (and does not appear to have been intended to do so) the peculiar binding character that is the hallmark of distinctively moral relationships. I propose an alternative account in which the concept of truth as a partnership among human beings has a central place; and I claim that it *can* establish a linkage between the reciprocal character of our disclosure of one another and primary moral notions such as responsibility and trust.

In Chapter 3, I argue that *Mitsein* is not only the ground of ethics in a positive sense, but makes possible a distinctively human wrongdoing and a special kind of evil as well. I also propose a theory of the good that goes altogether beyond anything that can be attributed to Heidegger, but is consonant, I argue, with the conception of *Mitsein* as the ground of ethics. Finally, in the Conclusion, I sketch some possible adverse reactions to the theses of this book; I then take up the conception of a ground of ethics, which turns out to be central to these otherwise very differently motivated criticisms. The point is made that a ground of ethics, as I conceive it, is a distinctive relation between human beings rather than a supreme moral truth from which rules of conduct could be deduced. I also discuss briefly how a theory of being as presence that makes a place for *Mitsein* is relevant to the situation in which humanity finds itself in an age of science.

II

This agenda is in marked contrast with normal practice in ethical theory at the present time. It is very noticeable that, for most contemporary writers on these subjects, the concept of a human being does not appear to be problematic in any philosophically interesting way.[9] Most notably, the whole topic of the status of human beings as subjects is typically left aside or dealt with only in the language of common sense or some appropriately naturalistic variant thereof. It would seem that a fear of straying into some forbidden "metaphysical" domain is a principal motive for this attitude. However that may be, the result is the peculiar featurelessness that commentators have sometimes noted in the way the human beings who figure in contemporary

---

9 It is true that there has been a good deal of interest on the part of English-speaking philosophers in the concept of "person" in recent decades; but this interest is largely independent of the ontological issues that arise in connection with the concept of human being, or *Dasein*, as it is understood in Heidegger's thought.

ethical theories are conceived and presented.[10] As I will try to show, a reliance on common-sense understandings in the context of such inquiries as these has its own hazards; and it is by no means clear that, for all their familiarity, these understandings are any less "metaphysical" than the revisionary alternatives to them that are so severely deprecated. In any case, the account I will offer attempts to show that an ontology of human nature is of fundamental importance to any effort to get at the ground of ethics.

The assumption on which I am proceeding is thus that it is the special character of the *relationships* among individual human beings that is of central importance for moral philosophy. This may seem to be a very banal remark because one would naturally suppose that the history of ethical theory must be that of an effort to understand just those relationships. And yet there is a difference here to which attention needs to be drawn. In general, these relationships have been understood to be those holding between persons who are all subject to the same body of ethical principles or rules. These have been variously conceived, sometimes as necessary a priori truths, sometimes as the terms of a social contract, and so on. In the latter case, the relationship in question is understood as that of people who have in effect made reciprocating promises to one another. That represents an important insight; and I will have something to say about the practice of promise-making in the course of my own discussion. But promising, whether express or tacit, is only one element in the larger relationship with which I will be concerned.

That relationship, which does not emerge with any real clarity in the ethical theories with which I am familiar, is the relationship between one human being and another simply as beings that are in the world together with one another. The mode in which they are in the world together is that of *disclosing* both other entities and themselves.[11] It is this Heideggerian concep-

10 This seems to me to be true of both the two major reconstructions of moral and social thought that have been attempted in the postwar period: those of John Rawls and Jürgen Habermas. It is certainly legitimate to abstract, as both these authors do, from the personal characteristics of the people that they are talking about. It is something else, however, to set aside all questions that have to do with the generic relationship of one human being to another and the bearing of that relationship on ethical matters. In the absence of any attention to such issues, the ultimate authority for the social arrangements these authors propose would be entirely a matter of the contribution they make to the well-being of the people who adopt them. It is deeply problematic, in my view, whether such a basis for ethical theory can ever yield a strong concept of obligation. In Chapter 3 I try to show the difficulties that such an approach encounters.

11 The word "disclose" translates the German word *entdecken*, which Heidegger uses extensively. *Ent-decken* might also be translated as "un-cover" or, indeed, as "dis-cover." In all these English words there is a prefix – "un-" or "dis-" – that negates the idea expressed in the rest of the word. This is the idea of something being covered or closed off and thus by implication hidden. This is true of the German *ent-decken* as well. All these verbs, therefore, describe human beings – *Dasein* – as negating the covered-upness of entities (*Seiendes*) gener-

tion of a human being as a "subject-entity" (*seiendes Subjekt*) that makes the character of our being together in the world much less "obvious" than it is usually thought to be. For among the entities that are so disclosed are not only things or objects whose mode of being is quite different from that of the *Dasein* or ek-sistent being that discloses them, but also other like entities – other human beings.[12] This means that this kind of entity has the distinctive feature of turning up both as self and as other. More concretely, both Ego and Alter and all their cousins not only *have* a world in the Heideggerian sense, but are reciprocally present to one another as having a world – the same world – in a way for which there is no really convincing parallel in the natural world.[13] It is this relation of reciprocal presence that Heidegger calls *Mitsein;* and it is entities standing in this relation to one another that he says are "for the sake of others" – that is, for the sake of one another.

This relationship is so familiar to us that we rarely, if ever, stop to consider it or give it a name; this is presumably the reason why not very much attention has been given to it by moral philosophers. In part, this has been due to a deeply ingrained belief that ethics should be independent of both empirical and philosophical theories of human nature. One can sympathize with that attitude since all too often such theories have themselves incorporated

ally and thus bringing them into a zone of openness that Heidegger also calls *Unverborgenheit* or unhiddenness. A distinctive feature of human beings is that they can reciprocally disclose one another whereas their dis-closing of things is not and cannot be so reciprocated. The relation of human beings to animals is in some sense reciprocal but presumably also impoverished by comparison to that of human beings to one another.

12 There has been much controversy about the status of the concept of a subject in *Being and Time* and in Heidegger's thought as a whole. It is clear that he rejects the notion of subject in its traditional form as the concept of a mental substance that contains representations of "external" objects. At the same time, however, Heidegger calls *Dasein* – his concept of the kind of entity that a human being is – a *seiendes Subjekt* – a "subject-entity." It is the confusion of these two senses of "subject" that has caused some readers to conclude that the concept of subject is simply eclipsed in Heidegger's thought. All these matters are discussed in detail in my *Heidegger and the Philosophy of Mind* (New Haven: Yale University Press, 1987); and especially in my article "Being, Truth and Presence in Heidegger's Thought," forthcoming in *Inquiry* 48 (1998), no. 1.

For an explanation of the term "ek-sistent," see Chapter 1, note 3.

13 The concept of presence is a central one in this book and so a further word of explication is in order. This is the most general concept that Heidegger uses to express the status of an entity that is (or has been or could be) disclosed – that is, perceived or remembered or expected – by someone. Most importantly, its being present or present in absence in one of these modes to someone is what is expressed in the name *Dasein*, which Heidegger gives to the kind of entity that can disclose another entity and/or itself in its being in such a way that it may be said to be present to it. Because any assertion of the being of an entity involves its being present to the perception or imagination or memory – these are our psychological designations of what Heidegger calls disclosure (*entdecken*) – of the entity that makes this assertion, Heidegger describes presence as the fundamental character of being as such. For a discussion of the sense in which absence can be a form of presence, see my *Heidegger and the Philosophy of Mind*, ch. 3, "Presence and Absence."

unacknowledged ethical assumptions of one kind or another with the result that the arguments founded on them take on an unhelpful circularity. But there is also (and perhaps more influentially) a belief at work here that there is really nothing about being in the world with one another that is not simply self-evident and thus unproblematic. If that is true, then everything about this relationship must have been noticed long ago, and the idea that on closer scrutiny it might reveal something of philosophical importance must appear very implausible.

On the view of human nature that finds favor at the present time, it is typically the rationality of these human beings who live side by side with one another that is held to be the proper object of philosophical interest. What is objectionable in this is not the emphasis placed on rationality as such, but rather the peculiarly discarnate and contextless way in which rationality itself is conceived.[14] This is well illustrated by a pervasive principle of method that substitutes the "logic" of ethical discourse and the logical relations among characteristically ethical statements for any characterization of the relations between the people who make them that goes deeper than our ordinary common-sense observations. Plainly, such a view of the business of ethics is abstracted from situations in which one human being confronts another and has to justify what he does to that person as someone who is affected by it.[15] My contention is that when the fuller context of such justificatory activity is borne in mind, many things that might otherwise be missed become available for philosophical reflection. In this way, moreover, the supposed obviousness of everything about that relation begins to look quite dubious. In any case, it is surely the business of philosophy to question the "obviousness" of many matters that other disciplines pass over quickly on their way to ostensibly more important areas of inquiry.

My thesis, then, will be that our being "for the sake of others" does indeed follow from *Mitsein* as this relation of reciprocal presence. This does not mean that I am proposing to pull a list of specific "dos and don'ts" out of the argument of this book. The underlying thought here is rather that in an important sense the recognition of another human being as complementing one's own being is prior to the definition of such substantive rules of conduct, whether of justice or whatever, and that this identity of Ego and Alter, accordingly, needs more attention than it has received in ethical theory.

---

14 At least a minimum of what we call rationality is implicit in the concept of disclosure itself. That is, an entity is always disclosed "as" something – typically as something that can be used in a certain way – and as such its status is such that it could (though it need not) be referred to in a statement. It is susceptible of the various "logical" transformations that that entails and that are expressed in the temporal and modal features of what Heidegger calls interpretation.

15 Throughout this book, "he" and related pronouns are used in referring to hypothetical persons of either sex.

More concretely, I want to show that as a consequence of this identity every human being has, simply as such, a claim on us to be included in the class of those to whom whatever ethical principles we acknowledge are applied – the class in which we ourselves are conspicuously included. The basis of this argument will be the thesis that, implicit in this reciprocity, there is a kind of partnership among human beings and that this partnership carries with it a binding character of a specifically ethical kind. It follows that if we are to understand the nature and authority of the ethical relations generated in this way, we must have a better understanding of the fundamental ontological condition of human beings – that of being in the world with one another. By using the concept of *Mitsein* as my guide to that understanding, I hope to be able to provide a sound philosophical basis for the thesis that, to use language that has been proposed by K. O. Apel, the authority of the ethical is quite generally grounded in a "subject–subject" relation.[16]

The implied contrast here is with the more traditional view that conceives the ground of ethics as something "objective" – something that a human subject is supposed to be somehow unavoidably conversant with but that does not otherwise have any special connection with the ontological character of "subject-entities." It is as though there were some objective fact or truth that could guide each one of us to the right ethical conclusions and thereby give our *Mitsein* the ethical character that it would otherwise lack. As I pointed out earlier, this view yields the conception of the ethical relationship between human beings as established by our all being subject to the same body of ethical principles, which for these purposes count as "objective." But my contention will be that there is a relationship in which we stand to one another that is in some sense prior to all the substantive ethical rules under which we live and that it is this relation that constitutes the ground of ethical authority. Instead of being reduced to the status of a neatly packaged object of apprehension, the ground of ethical authority has to be understood in terms of a dialectic of human agents under conditions of *Mitsein*.

The nature of that dialectic will be set forth in the chapters that follow; and it will be made clear there that it does not require any special powers of intuition such as theories of special value properties have seemed to presuppose. In order to avoid these spurious issues concerning the "objectivity" of moral facts, I make the relation of one subject-entity or *Dasein* to another the crux of my argument while still making a case for the authority of moral requirements. Admittedly, all these terms (and especially "subject" and "object") have been used in so many different ways that the formulation I have just offered may not convey very much. In some cases, it may even

16 See Apel's discussion of the whole objective/subjective issue in *Toward A Transformation of Philosophy,* translated by G. Adey and D. Frisby (London: Routledge and Kegan Paul, 1980), especially the essay on "The Community of Communication and the Foundations of Ethics."

prove misleading, because "subject" goes all too naturally with "subjective" and the usual connotations of that word are especially inopportune for my purposes in this study. I hope that all this will become clearer as I go along. What I can say now is that in speaking of a subject–subject relation, I am presupposing a quite different (and much more Heideggerian) sense of that term than the one most widely employed in the main philosophical tradition.

There is one other point that I should like to make here. There is a long-standing tendency on the part of pretty well all of us to think of ethics as something that is imposed on us from without. At one time, this idea was linked with a disposition to take a very dim view of our own human, all-too-human nature as the source of resistance to a perfect compliance with what is required of us by our maker. But even now when that idea has lost much of its appeal, there is still a tendency to identify ethics with images that are associated with such an absolute and external source of the ethical constraints on our lives. My own guess is that in this way a kind of latent antipathy to the whole business of ethics finds expression and, in a *faux naïf* sort of way, claims to be speaking in behalf of a much vilified but essentially decent human nature. What both parties to this controversy do not appear to understand is that this human nature that the one denigrates and the other defends is neither hopelessly corrupt nor spontaneously benevolent. The idea that it has to have the substance of its ethical life imposed on it from without has as little to recommend it when it emanates from a genuine belief in the corruptness of our own natures as when it comes from an unavowed desire to discredit the whole notion that obligation – being bound – has any place in this story. What is true is that we are unavoidably implicated in ethical relationships with one another and that in those relationships we are both bound and free. We are bound because we cannot claim a right to treat others in a way we could not accept for ourselves. We are free because it is only in our relation to others that we can acknowledge and realize our own human nature.

What I am suggesting is that in our everyday thinking about ethics we tend to be caught between an inflexible legalism and a self-indulgent antinomianism that can make even the old rigidity seem welcome by comparison. Plainly, such a cycle leads nowhere; and so it is not surprising that there has recently been a disposition on the part of many philosophers to give up the search for an ultimate ground of ethics altogether. The alternative would be to make do with such intuitions as we have of what is reasonable and unreasonable in the field of conduct without requiring that they be authenticated in any deep philosophical way. My view is that, in spite of the spotty record philosophers have made in seeking a ground of ethics, the search should not be simply given up, and that there are still alternatives to the classic rationales that have not been adequately evaluated.

One of these is the idea that instead of searching for something mysteriously remote from the common business of life we need to look more deeply into human sociality itself and to do so in a way that is informed by a more adequate philosophical anthropology than the one current in the social sciences at the present time. This is where the Heideggerian concept of *Mitsein* comes in; and my hunch is that a philosophical account of *Mitsein* can help us to achieve a better understanding of the sense in which we ourselves may be said to generate the constraints to which we are subject. The strategy of argument here would be to show that since we contribute to their constitution (and rely on them vis-à-vis others as well) and do so by virtue of the kind of entity we are, we cannot very well repudiate them, explicitly or implicitly, without serious incoherence. If it seems improbable that a concept as exotic as that of *Mitsein* could have that kind of relevance to our lives, I would reply that, for all its surface unfamiliarity, it deals with matters of which all of us arguably have a certain understanding, however inarticulate it may be. The task is, accordingly, one of finding a way to make something that is so familiar to us that it does not appear to require any closer scrutiny yield its relevant implications for the purposes of this inquiry.

III

There is a special difficulty that faces any attempt that, like this one, seeks to demonstrate the ethical relevance of Heidegger's thought. The principal occasion on which Heidegger took up questions about society and political life and tried to apply the existential concepts he had previously developed to this new domain was his Inaugural Address as Rector of the University of Freiburg in 1933. To his everlasting discredit, he used that occasion to associate the idea of a collective authenticity with the prospective reconstruction of German society under the leadership of Adolf Hitler. This stand, together with Heidegger's failure in the postwar period to acknowledge the criminal character of the regime with which he had associated himself and his thought, has understandably done immense damage to his reputation. In these circumstances, many will think it very strange and even offensive to suggest that his thought may nevertheless prove fruitful for the purposes of ethical theory.

That is, nevertheless, the claim that I want to make in this book. In my view, it is quite unjustified to conclude that *Being and Time* or, for that matter, Heidegger's other philosophical works must be tainted by the indefensible political stand its author took.[17] One has only to ask, with respect to

17 In the most considerable effort to establish a continuity between Heidegger's philosophy and his Nazism, Richard Wolin's *The Politics of Being: The Political Thought of Martin Heidegger* (New York: Columbia University Press, 1990), much is made of the fact that Heidegger claimed that it was the concept of historicity that set him on a track of thought that led to his affiliation with the Nazis. But there is an obvious difference between the kind of sense

any of the leading concepts of that book, like being-in-the-world or readiness-to-hand or temporality or historicity, what their political implications are to realize that there is no defensible answer to this question. What is true is that when Heidegger began, in the early 1930s, to try to connect the ontological analyses of *Being and Time* with the larger themes of history and society and the state of humanity generally, his thought began to take on a prophetic quality that had been notably absent up to that point and that was recognizably similar to the right-wing orthodoxies of the German professoriate of his time as well as to elements in his own personal background as well. He also apparently convinced himself that Nazism was somehow convergent with his thought about the world-historical crisis in which he saw humanity as being involved. This says more about his ignorance of the political world and his capacity for self-delusion than it does about anything that can be said to derive from his account of being as presence or human being.

Heidegger is not the only great philosopher whose conduct in the arena of public affairs has been contemptible but who nevertheless made important and original contributions to thought. Although we inveterately want our heros and villains to be all of a piece, that simply is not the way things work. In this respect, philosophers can be just as disappointing as the rest of us; and the associations of philosophers, beginning with Plato and Aristotle, with the world of power have always been suspect and their judgments often deplorably misguided. In our own day, to cite just one example from the other end of the political spectrum, Sartre was apparently unable to recognize the Communist regimes of Eastern Europe for the tyrannies they were. But if this fact is irrrelevant, as I think it is, to an assessment of *Being and Nothingness,* how can Heidegger's implication in Nazism dictate a judgment on *Being and Time*?

Heidegger made of his own and Germany's past and a philosophical thesis about our historicity, like the one in *Being and Time,* that says that we always understand our lives and our time in terms of a certain way of configuring the relationship of our past – the past of our community – to the present and the future. Nor is Wolin any more successful in showing that the central ontological concepts of *Being and Time* have a political dimension. What does emerge from the account he gives is that his own understanding of that work permits him to speak of "the quasi-solipsistic, Kierkegaardian theory of subjectivity advanced in *Being and Time*" (p. 102). The concept of being-in-the-world has nothing to do with Kierkegaard; and if there is anything that Heidegger never even came close to, it is solipsism.

On the attitudes prevalent in the German academic world of Heidegger's time, see Hans Sluga, *Heidegger's Crisis: Philosophy and Politics in Nazi Germany* (Cambridge, Mass.: Harvard University Press, 1993).

1

TRUTH AS PARTNERSHIP

I

Jürgen Habermas has argued that the approach of philosophers to almost every aspect of knowledge and inquiry has been conceived in what he calls monological terms.[1] This means that the *logos* of things – the rational principle that makes their existence and nature comprehensible to us – is something that we possess, to the extent that we do so, as individuals and not jointly or collectively, at least in any essential way. In support of his thesis, Habermas might well have pointed out that in the eyes of many philosophers even the epistemic relation in which we stand to one another has appeared far from secure. These philosophers typically construe the issue posed by the claim we make to have knowledge of the existence of other intelligent beings like ourselves as what they call the "problem of other minds." In such an approach, the philosophical inquirer is assumed to be already situated in and familiar with a world that lends itself to the kind of comprehension that eventually finds full expression in the sciences of nature. At the same time, however, he is supposed to be in a position that enables him to raise doubts as to whether there is any other being that is like him in this respect.

1 For an account of Habermas's wider conception of inquiry and its social character, see his *Knowledge and Human Interests*, translated by J. Shapiro (Boston: Beacon Press, 1972), pp. 43–63. In many ways Habermas has been a strong proponent of the significance of *Mitsein* for philosophy generally, but only when it is conceived in linguistic terms. I have discussed this aspect of his work in my paper "Habermas As a Philosopher," *Ethics* 100 (1990), no.3, pp. 641–57.

Not surprisingly, this "problem" proves to be insoluble when posed in these terms. In the circumstances that are being presupposed, anything I can point to in the world as an index of the presence of other beings who, like me, can perceive and think and remember is itself part of the world as a self-contained system of objects. As such, it can provide no justification for postulating the existence of something as radically different from it as a "mind" is supposed to be. What is implicit in all this is the idea that the very existence of other beings like ourselves is somehow deeply problematic and that "other minds," and thus other human beings, are at best ultra-elusive, if not absolutely out of reach. But this picture in turn reflects an assumption that anyone who poses this question is evidently making about himself and that is itself at least as problematic as the existence of other minds is supposed to be. What it implicitly assumes is that this individual inquirer can look out upon the world as though he were simply trying to settle a factual question – Are there other minds? – and as though he could, at least in his capacity as an inquirer, live with one answer to that question as well as he could with the other. It is as though the attempt to find an answer to this question were a terrestrial version of Project Ozma, the only difference being that the big question, Is there anybody out there?, is addressed to our immediate environment rather than to outer space.

Unfortunately, this entails a further incongruity that stems from the fact that this philosophical inquiry itself is, in its modest way, a collaborative undertaking involving many participants who address their insights to one another in books and articles as well as face to face. In these somewhat surrealistic circumstances, it is hard to see what answer to their question these philosophers can expect other than the one to which they are already committed by the presuppositions of the "search" in which they are ostensibly engaged. The real point here is that it is impossible to have unfeigned doubts about the existence of other beings like ourselves. But even when this is at least nominally conceded, our ways of thinking about one another may still betray many of the tendencies just noted. In legal and other contexts, for example, we often hear people say that no one can look into another's mind – sometimes, more picturesquely, into another's head – and thereby determine what thoughts are motivating his conduct. The suggestion is thus that there is an absolute barrier separating the mind as a zone of privacy from what is in the public domain; and this is at bottom the same picture as the one that creates the problem of other minds. What reason can anyone have, after all, for postulating the reality of something that is supposed to be so effectively secluded from public view? The paradoxical consequence of this line of thought is that even if we are indeed in the same world together with one another, the language in which we describe our condition often appears to have been borrowed from a state of things in which we are not so sure about that. In these circumstances, the temptation to describe each of us as though he were in a world of his own can have great appeal; and so it is not surprising that an idiom that assigns to each of us just such a private world has achieved the considerable popularity it enjoys today.

Plainly, the relation between two or more beings that are conceived in this way can only be an external one – that is, not one that is constitutive of the being of the entities in question. This is what Heidegger expresses by saying that, when conceived in this way, human beings are understood as existing "side by side" (*nebeneinander*) with one another. "Side by side" here connotes an external relation that is modeled on the one that obtains among the natural objects we perceive around us. These objects, which are typically adjacent to one another, may affect one another in various ways, but we still conceive them as distinct unit-entities with their own nonrelational properties as well as the relations in which they stand to their neighbors. This conception derives from the idea of such entities as substances – that is, as things that, in Descartes's famous formulation, need no other thing in order to exist. When a human being is understood on this model, both of the parts out of which it is supposed to be compounded – the body and the soul or mind – are conceived of as substances; and these coexist with natural objects (and with one another) in the kind of mutual externality that is entailed by this way of thought.

It was Heidegger's great insight that when a human being is understood in terms of this model, its way of being in the world is assimilated to that of the natural objects for which the concept of substance or thing appears to have been primarily designed. But when a mind is conceived as a mental substance – a "spiritual thing," as he puts it – as it must be under this dispensation, the result is that the distinctive character of perception and thought as the disclosing of entities in the world is fatally obscured and has finally to be dealt with, very inadequately, by means of a theory of representation.[2] It is worth noting here that just as the concept of a mental substance as a container for representations unavoidably generates the so-called problem of the external world, so in its application to the relations among human beings it issues in the equally specious problem of other minds. More concretely, the notion of side-by-side-ness expresses a sense that although there are indeed a great many of us and we are often at very

---

2 Our usual conception of ourselves is one in which we are held to be compound entities that consist of a mind that is somehow associated with a body. Our most distinctively human functions are thought of as going on *in* the mind, which contains the representations of things in the world in terms of which we think. Unfortunately, this notion of ourselves as a kind of private inner domain generates any number of paradoxes having to do with our access to a world that, in this idiom, has to be thought of as "external." In these circumstances, the status of our knowledge of the existence of other human beings also becomes highly problematic.

close quarters with one another, each of us is, so to speak, in business on his own. Among other things, this means that the goals of our active concerns are in principle distinct from one another even when, as is often the case, they are qualitatively the same.

Even when this picture of our relations with one another is accepted, however, it need not be interpreted so strictly as to exclude altogether the possibility of cooperation among us. Cooperation can, after all, be in the interest of both parties, provided that each one keeps his own separate ledger of the profit (and loss) that may result. More specifically, in a less tangible but no less important form, such cooperation can extend to epistemic matters. All our specifically human undertakings – mine and yours and everyone's – are predicated on the availability to us of the information we need in these undertakings and thus on what is held to be the case in the relevant sectors of the world. In other words, both in the ordinary business of everyday life and in contexts of organized inquiry, we must always rely on knowledge that is already in the public domain. Such knowledge comes to us from many sources – word of mouth, textbooks, the instructions that accompany the new stereo we have just bought, and a thousand other sources. As a practical matter it is simply impossible for us as individuals to gather and authenticate every bit of knowledge that we need. We are, therefore, unavoidably dependent on others – other inquirers – for these purposes, and this means on the knowledge that has been accumulated over time by countless human beings who, for the most part, remain unknown to us.

These are indisputable facts about our epistemic condition; but in a monological perspective they are just facts – that is, contingent features of our lives that limit what we can hope to acquire in the way of knowledge by and for ourselves. They are contingent in the sense that they are held not to affect in any fundamental way the first-personal character of knowledge. In defense of this view, it may be pointed out that although in matters of cognition we stand in the complex relations of interdependence just described, we cannot simply borrow knowledge from others without any judgment on its reliability. That judgment, whether it is explicit or implicit, sound or unsound, pulls the borrowed material into the orbit of the life that appropriates it so that in each case "I" alone am responsible for deciding, finally, what is true and what is false. This responsibility is underscored when we find reasons to think that the information we are being offered may be defective in some respect. We may then put it to the test and try to determine on our own just how good it is. But even if no such test is made, the incorporation of such "knowledge" into a given individual's system of praxis presupposes a judgment by him on its epistemic value. By making that judgment, each of us becomes the responsible party in the whole transaction just as the monological view would have it.

II

It would not be difficult to show that there is at least something implausible about this conception of the social character of our knowledge as a merely contingent feature that does not in any serious way call into question the underlying monological picture. That picture requires us to suppose that it would be possible, at least in principle, to test every assumption of fact on which we rely in this way and that it is just the convenience of being able to rely on others to do this for us and our not having enough time (or other resources) to do it ourselves that explains why we in fact do not do so. A number of obvious considerations can be cited that cast doubt on this view. One of these is simply the effect produced by a failure of confirmation of some knowledge-claim of ours by someone in a position to bear witness, one way or another, to what we say is the case. When this happens, it is not just the willingness of others to accept what we have asserted that is adversely affected; we ourselves must at least entertain the possibility that we are mistaken and if adverse testimony continues to pile up, we will eventually have to abandon our knowledge claim. What this means is that no one of us is able to certify, simply on his own say-so, that something is the case although there are certainly circumstances in which, willy-nilly, we have to rely on one observer or witness because there are no others.

There is another consideration having to do with this business of observation or witnessing that supports the argument I am making. It has to do with the limits on the range within the domain of fact (and this means in both space and time) that can be attributed to any individual inquirer. More concretely, there is no way in which we can conceive ourselves as ascertaining facts that obtained before we were born or will do so after we die; and the same kind of limitation clearly applies to our ability to vouch for what takes place at some great distance from us during our lives. We may, on a transcendental view of the self, imagine ourselves to be a kind of tenseless *cosmotheoros*. Even so, the attempt to divorce this transcendental self from its lowly empirical cousin cannot keep the notorious plurality of the latter from accruing to the former. In the actual circumstances of our lives, moreover, all the information deficits that are entailed by this plurality and its attendant particularity would still be in effect. In other words, we necessarily remain dependent on the testimony of people whose spatial and temporal positions differ from ours. Here, too, we doubtless apply certain epistemic criteria like that of consistency to the testimony that comes to us from the past; but it certainly does not follow that we could "in principle" have gathered this knowledge ourselves. We are thus dependent, in this as in other respects, on others in a way that appears to reflect something much deeper about our epistemic situation than any practical labor-saving arrangement could be. But if that is the case, then this fact may well be a clue to an important and perhaps essential feature of our way of being with one another.

Still another counterexample would base itself on the existence of language as the medium in which any facts we discover have to be expressed but that no one of us can claim to own or to control in any unilateral way. Instead, the facts in which we deal are evidently tied to ways of cutting up the semantic pie that are not, to be sure, laid down a priori, as philosophers once thought, in some way that would be uniquely authoritative for everyone, but that must, nevertheless, be common to the members of any human group who communicate with one another in a given language. Even without entering into the controversy about the possibility of a private language, it does seem clear that it is *not* just a contingent fact about us that we use a language that is in the public domain in this sense. But in that case the way in which the states of the world in which we are interested are designed cannot be attributed to any individual designer as if they were his "originals." Instead, each of us is plainly committed to a shared system of meanings, and this fact is at least hard to reconcile with the monological picture of how we stand to one another as "knowers."

For reasons like the ones just reviewed, it seems to me that it would be more plausible to suppose that every inquiry, whether into the reality of other minds or whatever, presupposes the existence, not of a solitary self, but of one that is essentially embedded in a field of selves and that this fact is a prior condition for the achievement of the kind of epistemic mastery over an objective natural milieu that is presupposed in the picture I have been describing. But in that case it would follow that the disclosure of entities in the world that is the defining characteristic of an entity that, in Heideggerian parlance, "ek-sists" is essentially joint and cooperative; and this would mean that inquiry, generally, is at a very deep level a modality of *Mitsein*.[3] It also entails that the disclosure of objects by such a being must proceed *pari passu* with the (at least tacit) acknowledgment of other beings like itself. If so, the first and primary milieu of human life must be constituted, not as a self-contained system of objects, but as what Heidegger calls a *Mitwelt* – a milieu that is common to indefinitely many beings that are in it in the mode of having it as their world and, above all, are in it with others as these others are with them.[4] It is most emphatically not an "external"

---

3 Heidegger's decision to use the verb "exist" only in its application to human beings inevitably causes confusion. Consequently it seems best to use another form of that word, "ek-sist," as he himself sometimes does, that breaks it up into *sisto* ("stand" or "set" in Latin, a cognate of the Greek *histēmi*) and *ek* ("out" or "beyond"). In this way the root idea of transcending or going beyond that motivates Heidegger's use of the word is exposed and confusion with the usual senses of "exist" is avoided.

4 The usual conception of what is meant by the word "world" makes it the totality of all the entities that exist. On this view, each of us would simply be one of those entities. By contrast,

world nor, for that matter, an "internal" world either, whatever that might mean; and so far from having the status of some inferential beyond or thing-in-itself, it is the forum in which we are essentially *with* one another and not simply side by side in the way we conceive natural objects to be.

In order to avoid confusion, it may be worth noting here that some philosophers of an idealistic persuasion have held that finite selfhood as well as the plurality that goes with it is in some sense illusory and finally unreal.[5] This thesis has also been expanded into a conception of something like a fusion of particular finite selves into an over-soul or world-spirit that is then declared to be the ultimate reality. To the degree that a view of this kind draws attention, as it typically does, to the kinds of considerations that have been touched on here and that put in question the validity of a strict epistemological individualism, there is a measure of affinity between it and the view being proposed here. At the same time, however, these positions are very different from one another since the particularity and finitude that are inherent in the kind of entity – *Dasein* – that can be a party to *Mitsein* exclude any coalescence, however it might be conceived, of two or more such entities. Indeed, I think it would be best, in order to avoid the extravagances that might otherwise be associated with it, to view any such idea as a form of rhetorical overstatement, in the material mode, of a conception of *Mitsein* like the one to be proposed here. There are certainly differences between, say, Hegel's conception of *Geist* and Heidegger's account of *Mitsein;* but they both do much of the same work. In the medium of *Mitsein* as in that of *Geist* we may be said to complement (and confirm) one another in piecing out the being of the world. The difference is that in doing so we

---

Heidegger understands "world" as that in which one dwells as an entity that discloses other entities as well as itself. In this sense, the world is always an *Umwelt* – that is, that which surrounds the "clearing" (*Lichtung*) that each *Dasein* constitutes.

5 Although we associate this conception in the first instance with the absolute idealism of the nineteenth century, it actually has a much longer history. In antiquity Plotinus appears to have been the principal exponent of the doctrine of monopsychism, although he drew extensively on kindred ideas in both Plato and Aristotle. There is a distinction to be made here between epistemic identity – the idea that the objects of knowledge are the same for everyone – and an ontological version of the identity between two selves, which involves the claim that the one originates in the other and eventually achieves full union with it again. Although in one sense it is epistemic identity that is at issue in this study, I would also claim with Heidegger that epistemic identity itself has ontological implications, although of a very different kind from those that philosophers like Plotinus apparently had in mind. (See Philip Merlan, *Monopsychism Mysticism Metaconsciousness: Problems of the Soul in the Neoaristotelian and Neoplatonic Tradition* (The Hague: Martinus Nijhoff, 1969.)

In connection with this last idea of an original unity with a divine consciousness or mind and an eventual restoration of the unity of the one with the other, it appears that something very similar can be found in Jewish mystical thought – the Cabala – where individual human souls are conceived as "sparks" from an original divine source. See Gershom Scholem, *Sabbatai Sevi: The Mystical Messiah* (Princeton, N.J.: Princeton University Press, 1973).

remain, for Heidegger, quite emphatically finite as our being-toward-death attests. Then, too, the distinction between entities and their being is not somehow overcome or *aufgehoben*, as Hegel would apparently have us believe. A "difference" remains that, Heidegger says, marks the parting of the ways between these two thinkers.[6] Nevertheless, the affinity survives these differences, as it does the many efforts that have been made to caricature the philosophical motives that find expression in these doctrines.

But if the problem of other minds takes on a very different aspect when viewed in this light, there is also an implication deriving from what has just been said that will seem paradoxical to many. A great deal of effort has been devoted to the task of showing that the knowledge we have of one another as human beings – that is, as intelligent and purposive beings – is logically of a piece with the knowledge we have of the natural milieu we inhabit. This means that the understanding we have of one another and of the kind of beings we are must finally come down to explanations in which observed facts are subsumed under lawlike regularities that are not different in any logically significant way from those employed in the natural sciences. This thesis has been contested in the theory of action as well as in the analytical philosophy of history, where strong arguments have been presented for the priority of what is sometimes called "rational explanation" over the nomological-deductive model just characterized.[7] In a rational explanation, an action of a human being or some group of human beings is explained by showing that it represents a way of dealing with a certain factual situation with which the agent is assumed to be familiar and of doing so in a way that will either bring about some outcome that is desired or prevent another that would otherwise occur. Such an explanation does not rely on any major premise in which some law-like pattern of behavior is attributed to the agent as the basis for predicting what he will do. The nexus between premises and conclusion consists instead in the linkage between a particu-

---

6 See Martin Heidegger, *Identitat und Differenz* (Pfullingen: Verlag Gunther Neske, 1957), pp. 42–3. This is not to suggest that the concept of *Geist* itself is in any way required in the statement of Heidegger's position on this or any other matter. Jacques Derrida has argued a case for some such conclusion as this, apparently with the intention of showing that Heidegger's Nazi episode can be understood in terms of his growing commitment to the notion of *Geist*. It may be that in his Nazi period Heidegger's evocations of *Geist* become more frequent; but it is hard to see that this amounts to much when Heidegger's ontology at no point makes any use of this concept. See Derrida's *De l'esprit: Heidegger et la question* (Paris: Editions Galilee, 1987).

7 I have discussed this conception of historical explanation from the standpoint of Heidegger's account of historicity in *The Dialectic of Action: A Philosophical Interpretation of History and the Humanities* (Chicago: University of Chicago Press, 1979), ch. 4. Some scholars seem to think that the account Heidegger gives in this connection of tradition is the key to such ethical views as he may have; but it is plain that historicity presupposes *Mitsein* and that it does not yield any concept of moral obligation independently of it.

lar factual situation and a particular action as the appropriate means to a desired outcome.

Usually explanations of this kind are thought of as being offered by someone – typically, a historian – who is looking back on the events in question. Clearly, however, those who directly participate in such events also need to understand what other such participants are likely to do; and in this sense, rational explanations themselves inform the events that are being generated by the actions of these agents. But in that case the human beings who are capable of this kind of agency and who both understand others and are themselves understood in purposive terms must be antecedently identified as beings to whom this form of understanding is appropriate as it would not be to the natural events that may be taking place around them. In this sense, there would be a kind of community made up of those beings to whom such explanations would apply and who can themselves understand one another in these purposive terms. What I want to propose is that the kind of understanding that is peculiar to those beings who belong to such a community is not only distinct from the explanation of natural processes, as the proponents of rational explanation claim, but also has another kind of priority over the latter. This priority would consist in the fact that it is only by virtue of our having identified other beings like ourselves through a form of understanding quite different from the scientific model that the sort of partnership can come into being on which the whole enterprise of knowledge – scientific knowledge included – depends.

Since the idea I have just thrown out is likely to meet with strong resistance, I want to see if I cannot make it seem a little more plausible by setting it in a developmental perspective, even if this is only rather sketchily worked out.[8] As our lives are getting under way, our relation to other human beings is one of profound and unilateral dependence; and the beings with whom we are primarily dealing are ones defined by their capacity to satisfy needs that we cannot satisfy ourselves. Such a being emerges from the wider environment through the role it plays in the rhythm of our own felt needs; and this is to say that it is at first incorporated into our lives in a way that allows it very little, if any, independence from those needs and, indeed, from us. At the same time, however, this symbiosis can never be ideally harmonious

---

8 I would like to think that the account I give here has at least some affinity with the work of the British psychoanalytic school, especially that of Ronald Fairbairn. If there is such an affinity, it would derive from the revision of the Freudian theory of the libido that makes a much larger place for the child's experience of other people. It is, by the way, a great misfortune that the term "object-relations" should have been chosen to convey the distinctive character of this line of thought, since it assimilates human beings to just what they are not – "objects." My understanding of these matters has also been deepened by Jonathan Lear's *Love and Its Place in Nature: A Philosophical Interpretation of Freudian Psychoanalysis* (New York: Farrar, Straus & Giroux, 1990).

or complete; and we are put on notice from time to time that this extension of the self is also (and distressingly) other. It is, in other words, both so close to us as to seem part of us and independent of us in ways that we have to learn slowly and painfully and long before there are words to express any of this. At the same time as we are learning to acknowledge their otherness – the fact that, for all their solicitude, these beings are not, after all, fully at our disposal – we are also learning to accommodate ourselves to the independent rhythms of *their* lives; and in doing so we acquire ways of dealing with objects and situations that would otherwise remain opaque to us. This is the way we begin the process of learning about how things work in the world and in that process these same equivocally defined "others" play an absolutely essential role. Not only are they implicitly understood as beings who are dealing with the same world as we ourselves are and who thus see and hear what we see and hear; they also see more and farther and better than we do and are thus able to guide our explorations of the world in which we are together with them.

What we observe in our relation to those who preside over our early lives are actions; they are understood as actions because the changes of position or state that, in the objectivist idiom, are all we can observe in the bodies of other like beings are in fact understood in the context of our own needs and desires and then, gradually and reluctantly, in the context of those of these "others" themselves as well.[9] This is to say that we understand them pervasively in purposive terms and that in doing so we learn to understand ourselves as well. Typically, the actions in question will be those of giving or withholding something that we want; and we learn to give and to withhold in just such a way ourselves in our relation to these same persons (and others) who supply our needs. But to give or to withhold in this way presupposes a familiarity on the part of the agent in question with the relevant elements of the situation through perception, memory, and expectation – just such a familiarity as the young child itself is acquiring.

What this comes to is the fact that even quite early in our lives we are acquiring what can only be called an implicit understanding of the purposive ordering of our own lives as well as those of others. But this in turn gradually brings into being an (equally implicit) understanding of the kind of entity each of us is; and this, too, is something we achieve in our relation to other like beings. Although, as noted, all this occurs before we have any ad-

9 This point can be made more succinctly by saying that actions take place in the world and not in nature. This formulation, of course, presupposes Heidegger's way of understanding the concept of world as what one might call a domain of openness or a space of presence. If the distinction between "world" and "nature" is not maintained, then actions simply become another kind of event in a milieu in which people, like everything else, are merely side by side with one another. In other words, "action" brings in the whole constellation of concepts that are (wrongly) excluded when the side-by-side approach is adopted.

equate words in which to express what we so understand, it is what in philosophical (or at least Heideggerian) terminology is called our being-in-the-
world – the transcending of the envelope of the body toward other entities,
among them other like entities. It is, moreover, just this "ek-sistence" by
virtue of which we are primordially *with* the latter that supplies the necessary condition for all further understanding of the world we dwell in. In
some such way as this, then, the pairing of one's own being in the world with
that of a real or putative other becomes a constitutive element within all our
perceptions of, and thoughts about, that world.[10] It follows that when in
adulthood we pretend to wonder whether there are any minds other than
our own, we are in effect trying to call into question something that has en-
abled us to reach the point at which we can pose this question.

The balance in this pairing between Ego and Alter undergoes many
changes in the course of our lives, and as it does so, the element of identity –
Alter is Alter *Ego* – or that of difference – Alter does, after all, remain Alter,
no matter what – may predominate, but there is no way the one can absolutely prevail over the other.[11] What I am suggesting is that this pairing of
identity and difference is at the heart of our relation to one another; and to
make this point a little more concrete, it is worth taking the developmental
story a few steps further. As we mature and our relation to other human beings gradually approximates more closely to something like equivalence
with respect to the ability to make our way in the world without constant su-
pervision, there is a marked tendency for the "otherness" of other human
beings to become better and certainly more explicitly defined than is their
continuing affiliation with the self. As the sense of one's own competence
grows, other people come to figure in our lives as beings with whom we work
and whose consent often has to be obtained for certain purposes of our own,
typically in the form of an agreement or a promise. We can no longer simply count on their providing for our needs; they have, after all, their own
concerns, which not only claim their time and energy but may even be such
as to get quite seriously in the way of what *we* want. Increasingly, it is as

---

10 This is a point that Husserl makes in his own way in *Cartesian Meditations*, translated by Do-
rion Cairns (The Hague: Martinus Nijhof, 1967), p. 124. For Husserl, the crucial step in
the construction of intersubjectivity is the acceptance of other people's observations as essential to the constitution of the objects that we ourselves perceive.

11 A fuller account of this "dialectic of intersubjectivity" would describe the ways in which we
effectively elide the reality of other people when, for whatever reason, it does not suit us to
acknowledge that reality in its full range of implication. There is a real sense in which our
procedures in this connection can be called "unconscious," since we certainly do not recognize them for what they are. On the other hand, as is so often the case with matters to
which the word "unconscious" is applied, the skill with which we manage to avoid just the
aspects of this whole matter that we are not prepared to acknowledge shows a considerable
familiarity with the very features of personal existence of which we at the same time want
to stay clear.

though other people, and with them we ourselves, were independent and sovereign principalities with which one can, of course, negotiate and possibly even sign treaties, but with which there is certainly no underlying identity or preestablished harmony of interests on which one could count.

In some such way as this, the picture of all of us as living side by side with one another in a kind of mutual externality begins to emerge; and in such a picture, our relations with others become at best a species of bargaining between beings who typically do not acknowledge that they are bound to one another in any more fundamental way. And yet it would not be difficult to show that this system of prudential cooperation in which the lines separating what is mine from what is yours seem so well defined is itself abstracted from our underlying condition of *Mitsein* with which we remain unquestioningly familiar at the same time as we deny it any recognition within our official theory of the world. Even so, our world remains, in Heidegger's language, a much more extensive "clearing" than it could possibly be if it were not implicitly understood as a world we are in with other like beings who share it with us. The plain fact is that, at every step we take in whatever endeavor our lives may be devoted to, we are constantly supplementing our own observations and our own recollections from a common fund to which we all contribute. So profound is this dependency that the idea that we could draw a line demarcating what we ourselves have supplied out of our own resources from what we have drawn from the common stock is more than a little problematic.

Although this anonymous/public element in our lives is widely recognized at the present time, it is often seriously misinterpreted.[12] Two such misinterpretations may be briefly noticed here although without any attempt to refute them beyond drawing attention to the way they appear to undermine themselves. In one of these, it is as though an acknowledgment of the pervasive social element in our lives had reacted against the original ontological characterization of individual human beings as entities that disclose a world. This is replaced by a conception of the disclosive function that ties it to "shared social practices"; by this route it passes over into a kind of social and cultural determinism that reduces pretty well everything in our lives to social habit and makes disclosure entirely dependent on a common anonymous fund of know-how and know-that. This line of thought can even

---

12 I have in mind here a way of interpreting Heidegger's texts that assigns a much larger and more positive role to *Das Man* than is normally thought appropriate. The principal representative of this line of interpretation of Heidegger's thought is Professor Hubert Dreyfus; its fullest statement can be found in his *Being-in-the-World: A Commentary on Heidegger's Being and Time* (Cambridge, Mass.: MIT Press, 1991), in which he goes so far as to declare that "*Dasein* does not choose at all" (p. 318). I have responded to Dreyfus's interpretation in "Heidegger à la Wittgenstein or 'Coping' with Professor Dreyfus," *Inquiry* 37 (1994), no. 1, pp. 45–64. For further comments on this issue, see the last section of this chapter.

be pushed to the point at which the individuality – better, the individuated-ness – of such human beings is called into question. Inevitably, this has the effect of making it quite unclear in what sense there can be said to be *many* such beings in the world if it is the case that as individuals they do not dis-close anything.

This same emphasis on the priority of the collective can also lead in an-other direction. All disclosure is sometimes held to be culturally bound, with the result that any public or universal character it may be thought to have would be confined to a particular culture as defined by the semantic grid of the language it uses. What is true in this is that disclosure is expressed in terms that may be parochial in one way or another, but the tendency of this line of thought is all too often to reduce disclosure as such to the status of an internal feature of a language or a culture. This is especially likely when the concepts of language and culture themselves are not informed by an on-tology based on being-in-the-world. What needs far more attention is the way in which this kind of parochiality is overcome as disclosure is made available to a wider and wider group of like beings through the procedures of inter-pretation that Gadamer has studied so carefully, and especially the "fusion of horizons" (*Horizontverschmelzung*) that results.[13]

III

I hope that what has been said thus far has made it appear at least doubtful that there is a problem of other minds. I have argued instead that the pres-ence of other beings that are in the world in the same way we are is disclosed to us in a manner that, so far from being more dubious than the presence of natural objects, is a necessary condition for our being able to gain knowl-edge of the latter. But the same line of thought that has led to this conclu-sion can be extended in such a way as to yield a characterization of the way we co-ek-sist with one another. To this end, it will be helpful to give a more detailed account of the way in which human beings are in fact reciprocally present to one another in the mature stage of their development that I have just been describing. By "mature" here I mean that the otherness of other human beings – their separateness from us – is fully acknowledged even though we may lapse, as we all do, into ways of thought that substantially abridge the independence of these people from us. What I want to show is that even in this separateness we are bound together in a way that is dis-tinctive by virtue of the central place it makes in this relation for the world understood as a milieu of presence and as a domain of truth.

Our relatedness to one another has many modalities and some of them do not presuppose our being in the world in any special way but only, say,

13 Hans-Georg Gadamer, *Truth and Method* (New York: Seabury Press, 1975).

the familiar facts of location and motion in a common physical milieu. There are occasions when we collide with one another and generally affect one another as though we were simply two physical objects moving in the way physical objects universally do. But no one thinks that the laws of motion can deliver a full account of human behavior. A reaction against any such view can, however, go all the way to the opposite extreme. It may be suggested, for example, that a truly human relation between human beings is one in which, in sharp contrast with relations of merely physical proximity and contact, deep calls unto deep – that is, one soul or mind calls unto another. On such a view – the theory of empathy, as it is usually called – Alter's inner state would be reproduced by Ego through a special kind of intuitive divination and vice versa; and the understanding so achieved would constitute the basis for a distinctively human relation between the persons in question. Since the difficulties attendant on this theory have been persuasively set forth elsewhere, I will not say more about it here except to note that it is, in any case, far too intricate to qualify as an accurate account of what is involved in ordinary human encounters.

In such encounters, when Alter sees me – Ego – and identifies me as being like himself a human being, he understands me, not as another "mind" in some problematic relation to what is going on around it, but rather as a being that, among other things, sees and hears what he sees and hears and can, at least in principle, identify it as he does. All this also works the other way around as well so that Alter is understood by Ego in the same terms. In these two cases, moreover, what Alter understands about Ego is understood by Ego as well; and Alter is typically in a position to understand what Ego understands about Alter. None of this requires any special psychological feats on the part of either of these parties; and instead of being a paradoxical communication of one mind with another, the first understanding we have of one another is, as one might put it, routed through the world.

Language and language use are the most obvious examples of the way our relations with one another are shaped by this kind of transcendence. When we seek the cooperation of another human being in some undertaking in which we have an interest, we try to persuade him by bringing to his attention some state of affairs that has an assumed relevance to his willingness to work with us. We may remind him, for example, of a promise he made to assist us at some time in the past. Even when our intentions are coercive in character – a threat, for example, of dire consequences in the event of noncooperation – it is to that prospective fact as what is conveyed by something we say that our interlocutor must respond. All of this is so familiar to us that we may fail to notice how profoundly different a relation mediated by such a reciprocal understanding of what is said – that is, typically, of something that purports to be true – is from the processes we observe in the natural world. This is not because we are strangers to that world or inhabitants of some loftier sphere, but because we are in it as a milieu of presence and are thus familiar with the be-ing, in all its modalities, of the entities that make it up. It is, moreover, this fact about us that sets the character of the relation in which we stand to one another by routing it through the world as a domain of truth.

These are matters with which we are all, in one sense, familiar, and yet their significance all too often escapes us because we try to express the disclosive function of human being that is involved here in ontic rather than in ontological terms. This is what happens when disclosure is conceived in representational terms as something that takes place *in* a human being or in the *mind* of a human being. Once this idiom is adopted, it becomes almost impossible to do justice to the fact that we are all entities that are in the world in the mode of having a world – the same world – and that we are, as such, sharers in a common truth.[14] As I hope to show, however, even under the markedly unfavorable auspices of this mode of conceptualization, the complimentary character of our mode of being of which I have spoken survives. Not only do we transcend the limits of any substance, mental or physical, with which we may be identified in the theory we favor; we cannot help understanding this fact about ourselves either. Even though our official account points us in a quite different direction, we are unavoidably familiar with the way we are bound to one another by the presence to us of a world that is common to us all.

What has just been said can be clarified in the following way. When I encounter another human being, I must at a minimum perceive him as a being

14 An assertion of this kind is so unlikely to be accepted in the present climate of opinion that something more must be added. We are experiencing a revival of the kind of psychologism that Husserl so decisively refuted in the *Prolegomena* to his *Logical Investigations*. It is unlikely that Husserl could ever have imagined the lengths to which political motives could take the kind of psychologistic relativism he argued against. In the interest of "diversity," even the most basic logical requirements are being relativized to cultures and periods; and in this way the idea of a common truth is rejected on the grounds that it simply serves the interests of the dominant groups in a society. The only way such a thesis could be made good would be if the different groups that are contesting this issue really inhabited different worlds. As it is, they live in the same world and in some mode of communicative *Mitsein* with one another; and that is what all the fuss is about. In other words, they are addressing one another; and under these circumstances, any attempt by one side to exempt itself from the requirements of a common intelligibility can serve only disingenuous polemical purposes. The truth is that there is no African mathematics any more than there was a Jewish physics; and whatever is proposed as true has to be shown to be true for everyone and not just for some preselected fraction of our species. Then, too, the emphatic claims that are made by the partisans of relativism leave no doubt that they are understood to have a general validity that everyone should accept, no matter what the professions of their sponsors may suggest to the contrary.

who, in normal circumstances, sees me and hears what I say and also perceives the same objects that I perceive around us.[15] There are, to be sure, cases in which not very much more than this can be assumed. If, for example, my vis-à-vis was kidnapped and brought blindfolded to the place we are in, I will be familiar with what lies beyond the walls of the room and he will not be. Or, more plausibly, if I am a high officer in an army in which someone else serves as a common soldier, I will be in a far better position to predict what will be occurring in the next few days than he is. There are, in other words, all kinds of differentials of what we ordinarily call "knowledge" between any two people who are present to one another; and there may also be differences that are due to misapprehensions on one side or the other of matters to which they both have access. In all these cases, the element of difference – difference in what is disclosed by or to the one and the other – may predominate in the relation between these two human beings.

At the same time, it is evident that this kind of difference is quite unstable. What is not visible to someone at one moment may become so at another, and an erroneous perception is often susceptible of being corrected. And what someone has not been in a position to discover for himself he may very well be able to learn from someone else. There are, of course, cases in which the way things really are is not immediately evident to untrained perception; and in these circumstances the differences between those who have the relevant capacity to observe and those who do not will be more deeply based and less easily removed. When this is the case, there is sometimes a temptation to interpret these differences as indices of some constitutional incapacity on the part of those who lack the knowledge in question. It can even happen that, by reason of the way a society is ordered, it comes to have a stake in such differences and discourages efforts to overcome them. In extreme cases, whole groups of people as defined by various criteria may be refused recognition as having any capacity (and thus any right) to have a voice in the public consideration of certain matters. But no measures of this kind can entirely remove the sense that the class of persons who are capable of contributing to the determination of the truth about the world they are in is, in a quite radical sense, open.

Jean-Paul Sartre has given powerful descriptions of the way in which the presence of another observer can amount to something like a threat to the ordering of the world to which we are ourselves committed and about which

---

15 These verbs of seeing and hearing are drawn from the psychological vocabulary in which we typically express the fact of presence. They unquestionably serve a purpose and it is not easy to see how we could do without them. Nevertheless, the act/object model they implicitly propose for our understanding of perception and other "mental" functions can be shown to be misleading in certain important respects as I have tried to show in my *What Is a Human Being?: A Heideggerian View* (Cambridge University Press, 1995), especially in ch. 3.

we may have strong proprietary feelings.[16] Such a threat is, of course, only the obverse of the recognition that such an observer may also confirm what we already understand to be the case. The real point here is that both this threat and this promise stem from the fact that, no matter how great the differences between people may be, there is no way that the truth about the world or any part or aspect thereof can be definitively reserved for or confined to certain human beings and denied to others. What this means is that as we encounter one another, we must see in another human being someone whose observations are in principle relevant to a determination of truth (and falsity) in just the way our own are.

It is considerations of this kind that restore the balance between difference and identity in the relation of human beings to one another. They can be developed in another direction as well that is especially relevant to the concerns of this study when it is borne in mind that this other human being that appears within our world also sees *us* – that is, in any given instance, *me*. Here, too, Sartre broke new ground with his phenomenological description of "the look" of another human being and of the way the person who is looked at responds to that look.[17] Unfortunately, he chose to confine the account he gave to a situation in which the person who is looked at is engaged in an act – peeking through a keyhole – that is shameful, both in his own eyes and in those of others. Sartre also persists in holding that someone else's look reifies or reduces to the status of a thing the person who is looked at. Plainly, however, the whole context in which such an encounter occurs requires that it be one human being who is looking at another. The other cannot, therefore, really be a thing and certainly cannot be magically transformed into one by the looker.[18] He may, of course, feel helpless to appeal against the judgment on him that is implicit in the look of which he is the object; and he may express this helplessness by imagining that he has been captured in a kind of freeze-frame that seems to deny his capacity to be anything else and in that sense is the equivalent of a reduction to the status of a thing. Once again, however, it is clear that this sense of having been "reified" is possible only for a being that is *not* the thing to which he sees himself as being reduced in the look of another like entity. Indeed, any such claim on either side would be just as much an act of bad faith as would be the attempt – so brilliantly described by Sartre – to apply to oneself the categories that are appropriate only to things.[19] The idea that the gaze of the other automatically carries the truth about me and my action is simply a

16 Jean-Paul Sartre, *Being and Nothingness,* translated by Hazel Barnes (New York: Philosophical Library, 1956), Part III, ch. 1.

17 *Being and Nothingness,* Part III, ch. 1, section 4.

18 This point is effectively made by Martin Buber in *Das dialogische Prinzip* (Heidelberg: Verlag Lambert Schneider, 1962), pp. 274–5.

19 See *Being and Nothingness,* Part I, ch. 2.

reversal of the assumption that I alone can determine this. The one is no better than the other and it wrongly simplifies the encounter between two *pour-soi* into the encounter between a *pour-soi* and an *en-soi*. It may, for example, be the case that even though I am caught by someone else peeking through a keyhole, I can claim to be justified in doing this. The point is that this has to be shown in some person-neutral way.

The true significance our being in this way the objects of another's regard lies in a different quarter from the one to which the bias of Sartre's sensibility pointed him. It lies in the fact that what Ego is and does becomes part of Alter's world as well since that world is the same as Ego's. The state of affairs it constitutes for Alter is the same one that Ego is familiar with, although it is also different in the way that what is reported by saying "I did that" differs from what is reported by "F. A. Olafson did that." In this way, identity is once again associated with difference; and they come together because Ego cannot deny that what is in Alter's world is in Ego's as well, although the context provided for it by Alter's life may be quite different from the one in Ego's. What this means is that Ego's action has in some sense slipped out of Ego's unique control; what that action *is* can no longer be simply a function of its place within the context of purposes Ego has set for it. Since both Ego and Ego's action turn up in Alter's world and since Alter undeniably has the status, even in Ego's eyes, of a co-dis-coverer of what is the case in the world they share, Alter cannot be consistently denied a role in the dis-covering of what Ego is doing or has done even though Ego very likely thinks of this as something to which Ego has exclusive rights. Alter's role will be especially clear when the action in question affects him and his life situation in some significant way. It holds, moreover, quite independently of any subsequent question that may be raised about the criteria that are to be used in determining what the character of an action is. As will be shown in the next chapter, such questions become all-important when there is a challenge on something like ethical grounds to what Ego has done to Alter or the other way around. But at this point the issue being raised concerns only the emergence into some kind of public status of an action that up to this point has been understood by Ego only in terms of his own desires and hopes. The de-centering of his world that results can often be almost as hard for Ego – that is, for any one of us – to deal with as it was when we were small and had to accept that what was uniquely important to us might not be equally so to someone else.

This, then, is the most salient feature, for the purposes of this inquiry, of the reciprocity of presence between beings who are in the world as a domain of truth. The chapters that follow will substantially expand this brief preliminary characterization. At this point, however, one or two minor clarifications are needed in order to forestall misunderstanding. For one thing, I may have seemed to be assuming that all the transactions that take place between human beings have a face-to-face character and take place in a context of perceptual presence. That, of course, is by no means always the case; and I have not assumed that it is. There can be no doubt that, when we are in a face-to-face relation with someone else, the considerations I have cited take on a special concreteness that makes it harder (but, regrettably, by no means impossible) to refuse to honor the equivalent status of self and other. But, as I have tried to show elsewhere, perceptual presence is not the only form of presence.[20] Paradoxically, even absence can be a kind of presence. Alter, that is, may learn of what Ego has done by other means than directly witnessing it; and when Alter does so, Ego's action will figure in the world as Alter discovers it with just as much reality as it would if Alter had witnessed it. And this is a fact that Ego himself must reckon with as at least a possibility even if he tries to keep secret what he has done. All the elements of reciprocal presence are thus brought into play even when there has been no face-to-face encounter between Ego and Alter.

The other point has to do with the claim, implicit in my line of argument, that it is as agents that we figure in one another's lives and that our actions rather than any "inner life" we may be supposed to have constitute our being for our fellow human beings. But this claim immediately invites the following challenge. If the issue between Ego and Alter turns on what Ego has done and thus on the way his action is to be identified, may not Ego's motive – his reason for doing what he has done – count for something in that determination? But in that case, can we really say that that is something that is disclosed to Alter simply by virtue of the fact that Ego's action is so disclosed? If the answer to this question is no, it would appear that the only kind of ethical judgment that would be consistent with this approach must be one in which only the consequences of an action are relevant to the way it is to be characterized, for ethical purposes or otherwise. That may indeed be the case, but is it not a little strange that that issue should be decided even before the specifically ethical aspects of such situations have come into view? If we are to avoid that incongruity, it would appear that some allowance must be made for an element in our actions that cannot in any clear sense be said to be disclosed to others. But in that case we would have to concede that because motives as private or inner states of the agent may not figure in the reciprocal presence of one human being to another, the importance of such presence for our ethical relations with one another must be revised downward.

Much could be said on this subject and especially about the new set of difficulties that must face anyone who opts for this line of thought; but I am not going to undertake such an extensive discussion. Instead, I will confine myself to one or two observations that may put the alleged privacy of motives

---

20 See my discussion of this claim in *What Is a Human Being?* in ch. 3.

in a different light. For one thing, it needs to be recognized that in a great many situations it is possible to read off the only motive that really concerns other people from the action itself, the situation in which it is performed, and the effects it produces. Typically, such motives are not very mysterious – no more so, in fact, than a baserunner's motive is for trying to steal second base or an investor's for selling a stock. Sometimes we are truly puzzled as when a friend who seems to have much to live for commits suicide. And even when the immediate motive for some action is clear, we may wonder why the intended outcome is attractive enough to a given individual to make it seem worthwhile.

But the relevant point about such cases is surely that an elusive motive need not be thought of as being a private or inner state of some kind, as if that explained why it is not disclosed to others. To say it is private or inner always tends to suggest that it must be accessible to the person in question as it is not to someone else, and yet this very often is not the case either. What is called for in such cases is something like a life history within which the puzzling action can find a plausible context. It is certainly true that such life histories are not generally available to us, so the action in question may always remain unexplained. There is no reason, however, to think that such an account would deal in private states any more than ordinary ones do, and so these failures do not support the case for an absolute form of privacy. For most purposes, in the absence of evidence that an action has miscarried, it seems best to understand what someone has done in the light of what actually happens as a result of the action as well as the agent's reaction to that outcome.

To this, a somewhat more explicitly philosophical point may be added. The objection I am addressing here derives from a deeply rooted dualistic assumption that declares our bodies to be one thing and our thoughts, and thus our motives, another. But if this distinction is associated with the claim that we are able to observe only the bodies of other people and the movements of those bodies, then, so the argument goes, any inference to what the person whose body we are observing may be thinking or feeling must be largely guesswork. If it were accepted, this thesis would certainly put a large hole in the argument I am making here. I have argued elsewhere, however, that instead of being a compound of such disparate parts – a body and a mind – a human being is a unitary entity whose mode of being is that of ek-sistence.[21] But if, by virtue of its being the body of such a unitary entity, the mode of being of that body itself is that of ek-sistence, it will normally show what its "owner" is about in the actions in which that human being transcends itself toward certain outcomes. The bringing about of those outcomes is what we refer to, in psychological language, as the motivating rea-

---

21 I have defended this thesis in *What Is a Human Being?*, ch. 6.

son for what the person in question is doing. What this really comes down to is the fact that the body has to be understood in the context of being-in-the-world and not just as the physical system that physiology abstracts from that context. When this is understood, the perilous gap between the observable "outer" side of a life and the hidden "inner" side really disappears. This is not to say that it is always easy to understand what someone is doing. It can be very difficult, but, as already noted, not because anything is hidden in the way the dualistic argument supposes. It also needs to be emphasized that the prospects for understanding become noticeably brighter when we remember that speech has to be included in the "behavior" of the body to which we are allowed access, even though it can hardly be said to have the physical character that the body and its movements are supposed to have. Even when what someone says about what he is doing or has done is designed to mislead the listener, it regularly tends to give away just what it was meant to hide, as any experienced therapist can testify. The conclusion to which all this points is that while the privacy of certain thoughts and motives cannot be denied a certain role in our relations with one another, it is by no means the fatal barrier to understanding that it is sometimes taken to be.

IV

There is one further element in Heidegger's account of *Mitsein* that needs to be noticed at this point, because it has a strong bearing on any ethical character that *Mitsein* may turn out to have. It has to do with the way *Mitsein* itself is implicitly understood by most people most of the time and by everyone at least some of the time. This understanding is at many points significantly different from the account that has been given in this chapter. Some things, of course, cannot be questioned; and among these is the fact that there are many human beings and that they are there for one another. What is possible, however, is for us, the entities that are in the world with one another, to give a good deal less than full value to the particularity of each human being that necessarily goes with that plurality. When we do so, we generate a mode of life that implicitly denies certain features of our own being, although it does so in a way that is in fact possible only for an entity that has those features.

It is in the domain of action and the discourse that is intended to describe or justify what we do (and do not do) that all this comes out most clearly. Probably as a result of the primary socialization that each of us has to pass through if he is to learn that he is, for many legitimate purposes, simply "another other," we may come to understand ourselves as being entirely subsumed under this essentially anonymous public identity. Heidegger studied this phenomenon, to which he gave the name *Das Man* after the impersonal "one" – the German *Man* and the French *on* – whose voice is heard in the utterances that are characteristic of this mode of selfhood.[22] These belong to a form of discourse that is inauthentic in the sense that, although ostensibly communicative in intention, what it conveys is not so much a real disclosure of what it is about, but rather a conventional version thereof that passes current in the anonymous floating palaver – what Heidegger calls *das Gerede* – of some human group. This does not mean that what reaches us in this way is false; its peculiarity is rather that it perverts "the act of disclosing into an act of closing-off" by making it appear that "things are so because one says so."[23] In other words, everything that needs to be disclosed has already been disclosed although without its being clear by whom or how. Nor is this simply a peculiarity of the communicative relations among the members of a human society. As Heidegger presents it, it forms part of a mode of human life in which an acknowledgment of the personal and individuated character of both presence and choice is systematically avoided or detoured around.

Such tendencies as these might seem to be most natural at a level of social development at which the idea of the individual and his cognitive and active powers has yet to emerge with any real distinctness. In Heideggerian terms, this would mean a mode of human life in which an acknowledgment of the personal and individuated character of both presence and choice is regularly simply missed, perhaps because it has not developed to a point that would make this impossible. This might bring to mind the kind of society we call "primitive"; but there is no reason to think that, in developing this concept, Heidegger had these societies primarily in mind. It would be a serious mistake, in any case, to suppose that the avoidances he describes are confined to an early stage in some postulated schedule of social development. Even in a society like our own that thinks of itself as being pronouncedly individualistic, our own version of *Das Man* maintains itself. It

---

22 Heidegger tells us that the status of *Das Man* is ontological rather than simply ontic; but he does not explain why this must be so. In a weak sense this might be the case because *Mitsein* has the status of an *existentiale* and *Das Man* is a modality of *Mitsein*. This would require, however, that the connection between *Mitsein* and *Das Man* be shown to be a necessary one; and Heidegger never does this. It might also be plausible to argue that because our *Mitsein* is marked by the finitude of our condition generally, we are unavoidably dependent on one another and on a more widely diffused store of conventional wisdom. This is the line I would take in explaining why we can never altogether divest ourselves of *Das Man;* but it is a quite different kind of argument from the ones Heidegger typically uses. On the other hand, to say that *Das Man* has an ontological status without giving a supporting explanation will almost certainly give the impression that *Das Man* is a strange kind of collective entity with a distinctive kind of being of its own; and this is an idea that Heidegger is on record as rejecting. I would suggest that an application of Sartre's analysis of bad faith to our relations with others would produce a more satisfactory account of the status of *Das Man* than Heidegger has given us.

23 *Being and Time,* translated by J. Macquarrie and E. Robinson (New York: Harper and Row, 1962), pp. 213, 212.

does so when the kind of anonymity and interchangeability that character-izes life in a mass society is extended to contexts in which it is not only out of place but markedly detrimental.[24] The result is a situation in which the concept of a human being as anything more than a nodal point in some much larger social network finds few takers, and a de facto transcendental status accrues to the presiding science-cum-technology that defines the workings of that system.

Under these auspices, the status of both what is "true" and what is "right" in the domain of action, like the "One" from whom it emanates, is that of an undefined publicity that makes it impossible to trace it back to any as-signable person who would bear responsibility for it. But an ethical relation is one that carries an assignable responsibility with it; and for that to be the case it would seem that the parties to that relation must at least be able to justify to one another what they do. But how, in the absence of such a rela-tion to one another, can there be a responsibility of one person to another? If the relation is to be an ethical one, it seems there would have to be some-thing like a partnership based on mutual acknowledgment between the two parties; and yet that is just the picture that is so difficult to apply in these cir-cumstances. Indeed, it is hard to see how ethical requirements could have any authority other than that of convention or any status other than that of the palaver in which they would be transmitted.

It is not surprising that under such auspices the whole disclosive function of language becomes deeply problematic, as does the very notion of a world that is prior to the process of "encoding" with which language is identified. There is, of course, no way this occlusion of presence can maintain itself consistently without a tacit acknowledgment of the very fact it seeks to sup-press. To the degree to which this is the case, the distorted form of com-munication to which this strategy gives rise may be said to bear witness to its own secondary and derivative character – that is, to the inauthenticity of its disclosive function. By "inauthentic" here I mean that because this kind of talk does not make a place for its own disclosive character, it cannot invite any co-disclosure of whatever it may concern by those to whom it is ad-dressed. Indeed, it is almost as though the intrusion of such an idea were

24 There has been a strong tendency in the contemporary world to violate the distinction be-tween the private and the public. Sometimes this has been done for its shock effect out of exhibitionistic motives, but more often it has occurred in contexts like that of advertising, where the evident intention is to associate some product with themes from the consumer's personal and domestic life. When people lend themselves to this kind of exploitation of their private lives, these lives really cease to be private and are instead assimilated to a sta-tus of public clichés. This is one aspect of what Jürgen Habermas has called "the coloniza-tion of the life-world" by interests that center on money and power; and it is in such ways as these that the style of *Das Man* seems to me to pervade wide sectors of modern life. See Jurgen Habermas, *The Theory of Communicative Action*, vol.2, translated by T. McCarthy (Boston: Beacon Press, 1997).

tacitly understood to be unwelcome. Arguably, the very efforts it makes to stay clear of the kind of disclosure that might undermine the false security it seeks to protect amount to an acknowledgment of disclosure as a function of individual human being.

It has been suggested that there is a positive aspect to this kind of anonymity because it amounts to an assertion of the authority of what is common in the way of knowledge and norms of conduct and thus of the nonprivileged character of any particular individual point of view. Such a thesis may even seem to be in the spirit of the argument made earlier about the need for the supplementation by others of the disclosure effected by any individual human being. There is a very significant difference between the two, however, since under the regime of *Das Man* the authority of what is public in the domain of knowledge is purchased at the price of a massive self-disqualification on the part of each individual human being. What Heidegger calls the perversion of "an act of disclosing" into "an act of closing off" is precisely the isolation of what is supposed to be the case in the world from the disclosive function of the kind of entity that each human being is. It is one thing for these individuals to acknowledge that they are members of an epistemic community and to accept the need for confirmation by others of their own surmises. To defer to the authority of an anonymous "one" that speaks in the voice of tradition and of conventional wisdom is something very different. As Heidegger points out, it entails, for those who do so, the acceptance of an ontological status that makes no place for either presence or ek-sistence and assigns to them the status of a thing and not that of a person.

This line of argument can be made somewhat more concrete by the following considerations. In the modality of *Das Man,* we do what we do because it is the done thing; and whenever we learn something from someone else, there is a sense in which our understanding of what is so learned is bound up with the anonymous authority of a shared practice to which the individual in question is our guide. In Heidegger's language, what this comes to is that there has as yet been no opportunity for an authentic disclosure by us – the learners – of the matter with which we are concerned. Fortunately, however, although this kind of situation recurs throughout our lives, it is also one that we can and often do move beyond. Thus, once I have learned to drive a car, I am in a position to grasp – to disclose – the reasons for a certain practice that I had accepted simply on someone else's say-so – in others words, in the mode of *Das Man.* The same could be said of countless skills in the repertory of any human group at a given time; they can be learned more or less by rote but later develop into an intelligent and flexible mastery of whatever equipment or materials they utilize. At that point it is no longer a matter of doing something because it is the done thing, which really closes off what it pretends to disclose. A similar point could be made with respect to customs that are observed in our relations with other people.

It follows that there cannot be any justification for placing an activity under the rubric of *Das Man* simply because it is part of the repertory of skills and technologies of a certain human group at a certain stage in its development. And yet this is what the philosophical patrons of *Das Man* want to do. It is as though the fact that in many situations I do the same thing as other members of my society (or perhaps of the human race) meant that I must be doing these things simply because they are the done thing. The most one can say in favor of this thesis is that our having to follow the example of others is a constant in human life if only because there are so many things that we do more or less blindly and never come to understand in any other way. To that extent, the thesis of the uneliminability of *Das Man* has a basis in fact but also a much more limited place in our lives than these philosophers suppose. What is most misguided in all this is the idea that one has to be original in order to be authentic. There is no basis for any such idea in what Heidegger says about *Das Man*. It looks very much as though the Heideggerian conception of *Das Man* has been confused with the more recent idea of "society" as an oppressive super-entity that tries to dictate or anticipate one's every move and leaves no space for anything that would express the distinctive character of an individual personality.

2

TRUTH, RESPONSIBILITY, AND TRUST

I

It would be an impoverished view of the relations in which human beings stand to one another that made these turn simply on a need for information in abstraction from any wider life context. That there is such a need and that it can be met only by a disclosure of the world that is both joint and co-operative was established in the preceding chapter. But by itself this kind of co-disclosure cannot generate an ethical relationship among human beings. For that, some conception of the interests and needs of these human beings is required and, with it, an understanding of how one human being can help or hurt another. In other words, instead of just talking about disclosure as such, it will be necessary to talk about action and its consequences and especially about the way the relation between human beings outlined in the preceding chapter informs the domain of human action. This chapter will deal with these matters as a way into the questions about how an ethical relationship comes into being between one human being and another. My strategy will be to try to determine whether there may not be a level of complementarity among human beings in the domain of choice and action that is modeled on but also goes beyond the complementarity of disclosure that was discussed in Chapter 1.[1]

---

1 The active nature of Dasein and the fact that things "matter" to it are primitive underivable characteristics of human being in this way of conceiving it. On this point, see my *What Is a Human Being?* (Cambridge University Press, 1995), ch. 5.

First, it will be helpful to clarify the way Heidegger understands the disclosive function of human being in its relation to action across the board.[2] Typically, we understand this relation in psychological terms: some desire or other on the part of an individual human being sets a goal and this goal is brought about by an action or a sequence of actions that is informed by knowledge of how this can be done. In this picture, human beings have two distinct sets of mental powers – the one cognitive and the other volitional and active – and these stand in a means-end relation to one another. At the same time, the relation between the end that is set by desire and the causal connections on which action depends is external in the sense that each of these terms can perfectly well be conceived in isolation from the other. This means that the design of the entities and situations in terms of which the field on which some action is to supervene is organized will typically be entirely independent of whatever active interest we may bring to it. This in turn presupposes that these entities and situations have been made manifest to us in a purely disinterested and unmotivated disclosure of what is in the world. That may not be a very plausible assumption, however, since, in the absence of a system of natural kinds, there is an indefinitely large number of ways in which the semantic design of the world or of any part of it could be construed.

Against any such view, Heidegger argues that it is precisely in our capacity as active beings that we disclose entities within the world at all.[3] This would mean that the disclosure that I have described as our transcendence of the envelope of the body toward other entities must always be another kind of transcendence as well – a transcendence *toward* something that we might bring about by taking action. On this view, disclosure is always associated, whether immediately or remotely, with a possibility of active intervention in the course of events; and, as such, it projects some future state of affairs rather than another as what is to be brought about.[4] In other words,

2 Heidegger's principal discussion of this topic and his exposition of the concept of readiness-to-hand (*Zuhandenheit*) can be found in *Being and Time*, translated by J. Macquarrie and E. Robinson (New York: Harper and Row, 1962), Part I, Division 1, ch. 3.

3 There is a question here about the status, in Heidegger's account of these matters, of theoretical knowledge and its relation to the kind of understanding (*Verstehen*) with which he is primarily concerned and which is closely tied to the active use we make of it. For insightful discussions of this point, see Gerold Prauss, *Erkenntnis und Handlung in Heideggers* Sein und Zeit (Freiburg: Verlag Karl Alber, 1977); and Carl Friedrich Gethmann, "Heideggers Konzeption des Handelns in *Sein und Zeit,*" in A. Gethmann-Siefert and O. Poggeler, eds., *Heidegger und die praktische Philosophie* (Frankfurt am Main: Suhrkamp, 1988). Both these studies reach the conclusion that the deepest implication of Heidegger's analysis is that even so-called theoretical knowledge is at bottom practical in character.

4 All these actions are purposive in nature; and Heidegger makes it clear that their ultimate *Worumwillen* – that is, that for the sake of which they are done – is the self as *Dasein*, the kind

since whatever is disclosed is disclosed in the context of a praxis that has a temporal horizon, it follows that the way the world is mapped expresses the interest we have in certain outcomes by laying out the routes by which they can be reached.

It is an equally important element in Heidegger's treatment of these matters that, in our typical mode of self-understanding, we pare away this context of action and possibility in such a way as to leave only the supposedly neutral states of affairs in the world and the decisions (or "values") that are spoken of as supervening upon them. In the Heideggerian conception, the context that is usually cut away is restored in such a way that disclosure itself is always understood to be tied to a project in which a sense of what things matter is implicit. More concretely, this means that the primary disclosure of entities is cast in an instrumental mode and envisages them in terms of what *can* be done with or for or to them. This is, if one wants to put it that way, Heidegger's pragmatism; but it is by no means prejudicial to an acknowledgment of truth as something we have to find and cannot simply invent.[5] So far from subordinating epistemic requirements to those of need or desire, this account makes an acknowledgment of the truth about conditional relationships among states of affairs in the world a necessary condition for effective intervention in it. There is, in other words, no sacrifice of the ability to take in the fact that some working assumption we have made is inapplicable to the purpose in hand and that it has, accordingly, to be appropriately modified.

It might, nevertheless, be thought that this interpretation of disclosure in functional and instrumental terms would be hard to reconcile with the claim that the world we disclose is one and the same for all of us. There is a sense of "world" – the one we appeal to when we speak of a doctor's world or a child's world – that allows us to speak as though there were as many worlds as there are categories of people who understand things in terms that are not shared by others. It should be noted, however, that even in this idiom doctors or scientists are not confined to these "worlds" that the rest of us are

of entity that *is* its future as much as it is its present and past. There is, however, no implication in this thesis that the self is to be understood in some narrow way that would automatically give everything we do a "selfish" motivation. The difficulty is rather to understand how we can be "for the sake of (*umwillen*) others" at the same time as each of us is the *Worumwillen* – the Wherefore or "sake" – of all his own actions. I am not suggesting that there is a formal contradiction here, only an unanswered question about how the self for the sake of which everything is done can be for the sake of others.

5 It has to be understood that if Heidegger is to be described as a "pragmatist," his pragmatism has nothing to do with anything like a "right to believe" – to believe, that is, otherwise than in conformity to the evidence – as did the pragmatism of William James, for example. Indeed, the concept of belief (*Glaube*) is one for which Heidegger has little fondness; and the reasons that motivate this attitude are discussed in some detail in my *What Is a Human Being?*, pp. 13, 55.

unable to enter. They also share with us a common-sense world of people and houses and gardens from which the kinds of entities and processes with which they are conversant ultimately derive. It is certainly much more difficult for us to share their world than it is for them to share ours, but it is by no means impossible. In the light of this traffic to and fro, it seems that it is still appropriate for everyone to postulate a single world that all of us inhabit even though it has many more facets than it may originally have appeared to have. We may not be primarily interested in the matters that require a specialized conceptual ordering of our otherwise common world but this does not mean that we are constitutionally disqualified for the task of retracing the steps by which such an ordering emerges.

If the epistemic and the active modalities of transcendence are associated in the way Heidegger suggests, certain things follow. For one thing, it means that the underpinnings of the classic argument that claims to show that "ought" cannot be inferred from "is" are themselves put in question.[6] That argument requires that the scene on which we look out be constituted out of brute facts – facts that have not been ordered in any purposive way and to which any suggestion of their incorporation into such an ordering would be quite alien. In fact, however, the first world we inhabit is, as Heidegger points out, a *Verweisungszusammenhangn* – a referential context – that has to be understood in functional and instrumental terms and only secondarily and derivatively in terms of facts that have been stripped of the kind of meaning that presupposes a setting of purposeful action and use. To put this in another way, the primary identifications we make of entities in the world we disclose are constituted as much in terms of possibilities as they are in terms of actualities. Because these functionally defined entities are already understood in terms of outcomes that are not yet actual, the appropriate picture of our situation in the world would be one in which we have to commit ourselves to one of the lines of action prefigured in these identifications rather than to another. It is not one in which we combine a neutral state of fact with the idea of something we desire and then gratuitously claim that there is some kind of universal warrant for this nexus that everyone must acknowledge.

To this it might be replied that, whatever the character of our "first" world may be, the "is/ought" thesis has to be understood as applying to a fully objectified world that is also, by definition, the real world. This equation of "real" with "objective" is itself highly problematic because it is invariably associated with a conception of the "mind" and of the "psychological" as a dumping ground for whatever does not find a place within the one real and

6 In saying this, I am in no way undermining the critique of the idea of a normative fact that was sketched in the Introduction. The fact that what is "given" is saturated with possibilities does not mean that any one of these possibilities is privileged in the special way that a normative fact would have to be if it is to make something the uniquely right thing to do.

objective world.[7] If that conception proves untenable, as there is every reason to think it is, we will have to think of the relation between our first world
and a fully objective one as a modification that *we* effect in the former by ex-
pelling from it everything that does not find a place in a preconceived par-
adigm of knowledge. In this way, everything is removed that might be hard
to reconcile with the absolute contrast between fact and norm on which the
concept of brute fact depends.[8] But in the kind of world that we disclose before we do this, the primary facts are instrumentalities – actual states of affairs understood in terms of their potentialities for realizing something that
is of interest to us. This is to say that there is already an element of concern
in our understanding of the makeup of our world and that our stance in that
world is from the outset one that has an active character that is reflected
back to us from the pragmatic ordering of the things around us. It is also evident that, in the context of *Mitsein* as a public milieu in which this interested involvement in the world has a plural character, there will unavoidably
be encounters and collisions between actions that follow the routes prefigured in the world. There will, accordingly, be the makings of a situation in
which claims are made to something like the priority of certain interests over
others – claims that, if sustained, would be expressed by an "ought." The da-
tum for ethical reflection is, accordingly, a number of (possibly) conflicting
claims to this status rather than a collection of brute facts and equally brute
demands.

7 It is still not as widely understood as it should be how closely the claim of the natural sciences
   to be "the theory of everything" is bound up with the validity of the operation that was performed on the concept of the world by philosophers in the seventeenth century and that has
   been, since that time, vigorously espoused by natural scientists themselves. This was the creation of the subjective/objective contrast and, with it, of the mind as the receptacle for mere
   appearance – that is, for everything that did not lend itself to the methods of inquiry of those
   sciences. Without that initial act of abstraction from "the world as we know it" and the availability of the mind as an *alibi*, an "elsewhere," for all the subjective debris that had been denied a place in the order of nature, the claim of the natural sciences to be *the* complete and
   authoritative account of what there is would seem feeble indeed.
8 "Removed" here must not be taken literally, since an actual removal of what violates the
   desiderated picture is beyond anyone's powers. It might be better to think of this operation
   as one of crossing out and, as such, rather like the way in which, in Heidegger's account of
   it, being as presence is crossed out by those who are blind to it. Certain features of our experience of the world are acknowledged but only for the purpose of treating them as not
   counting for the serious purposes of determining what there is; and the anomalous character of their status is dealt with by calling them "subjective." In this way, they are, in effect, assimilated to the status of something like mistakes in reasoning; and this means that they are
   not really there at all so there is no need to concern oneself with them. Merleau-Ponty has
   an excellent discussion of this whole strategy of what he calls "la pensée objective" in the
   Preface to *Phenomenology of Perception* (translated by Colin Smith [London: Routledge and
   Kegan Paul, 1962]). More generally, there is, he argues, an inference back from a preconceived idea of the objective order of things to what the character of the corresponding experience must be.

Another implication of this conception of the active character of disclosure is that in depending on others for information we are also depending on them for support in our active undertakings. It also follows that other people who assist us in the one respect, may well be assisting us in the other as well. This might suggest that Heidegger's conception of our "being for the sake of others" could be understood, at least in part, in terms of just such a relation of co-disclosure of the world. In other words, each one of us would constitute a resource for our fellow human beings through the disclosure of the world that we effect and that we make available to them on countless informal occasions of social life as well as in the context of organized inquiries. Nevertheless, plausible as this may seem, there is no indication on Heidegger's part that this resource has any special place in the conception of the aid we give one another that he sketches. Even so, there is a question here that needs to be considered: how would this kind of cooperation be possible at all if human purposes were hopelessly disparate and if no meaning could be given to the notion of a normative standard for these actions?

II

Under the rubric of human action there is a subheading for those actions that significantly affect other human beings and their interests. Unfortunately, this is not a matter about which Heidegger has very much to say. What he does say comes mostly in connection with the notion of *Fürsorge* – a word composed of *Sorge* (care), the central defining character of human being, and the preposition *für* (for). The natural translation might, therefore, seem to be "caring for." The drawback of that rendering is that it suggests that what Heidegger has in mind is principally a matter of doing things for other people. This is in fact what is conveyed by the English equivalent that has been used by the translators of *Being and Time:* "solicitude." This word has, I think, a narrower meaning than Heidegger intends – something like a personal concern that may be somewhat tinged by anxiety. That is, indeed, one kind of *Fürsorge* – the kind that Heidegger describes as being in the nature of an anticipatory response to someone else's needs so that he will not have to deal with them himself.[9]

As Heidegger describes this kind of solicitude, it almost seems to be in the nature of an attempt to free the beneficiary of such assistance from *Sorge* (care) as such. It thus stands in marked contrast with another kind of *Fürsorge* that attempts to help another human being but not by relieving him of the need to deal directly himself with the matters that are of concern to him. Heidegger does not give a concrete example of what would count as an instance of *Fürsorge* of this kind. He does say that it "helps the other to become

9 *Being and Time*, p. 158.

transparent to himself in his care (*Sorge*) and to be free for it."[10] And else-where he speaks of cases in which "I am responsible for the fact that some-one else is endangered, misled, or even broken in his life (*Existenz*)," al-though no law has been broken.[11] There may be a hint here of some kind of human solidarity that can be either honored or violated; but if so, it is not enlarged upon. In any case, it does seem that what Heidegger has in mind here would be better rendered as "caring about" than as "caring for." Un-fortunately, it remains a good deal clearer what this kind of *Fürsorge* is not than what it is. Certainly we are given no idea of what sort of claim on us ac-tions that come under either form of *Fürsorge* can have.

Before drawing any conclusions one way or another from this skimpy ac-count of *Fürsorge*, we must also take into consideration what Heidegger says in his account of conscience (*Gewissen*), especially as regards the concept of responsibility that is central to it.[12] He begins by invoking the traditional notion of the "voice" of conscience, but at the same time he insists that this voice is not that of God or of any supra-individual being. It is that of each individual human being, who is both the one that is addressed by it and the one it refers to. Conscience is, in fact, a kind of counterforce to *Das Man* – a form of pre-ontological self-understanding on the part of each human be-ing that is quite free of the everyday evasions that are so characteristic of that form of selfhood. It is the way in which each of us tells himself what kind of entity he is as a human being; and so its import is ontological rather than merely ontic. Heidegger is also at some pains to deny that conscience in this sense has what would ordinarily be called a "content" or that it is-sues specific directives or warnings to us. Conscience, he tells us, is silent and yet its very silence conveys to us something that is of the greatest importance.

What this silence conveys to each of us is the fact that although we live much of the time in the de-individuated mode of *Das Man,* we are never-theless individuals and as such are responsible, each of us, for what we do.[13] The issue this poses for each of us is whether or not we are willing to accept this fact about ourselves. To do that would require that we break with *Das Man* to the extent possible and be willing to recognize ourselves as being

---

10 *Being and Time,* p. 159. What Heidegger has in mind here sounds a good deal like what is sometimes referred to as "tough love."

11 *Being and Time,* p. 327.

12 The discussion of conscience and responsibility can be found in *Being and Time,* Part I, Di-vision 2, ch. 2.

13 It must be understood that Dasein is not *really* de-individuated in any sense that would make it impossible to say that there are many entities of the *Dasein* type. If that were the case, the concept of *Mitsein* would be meaningless since there would not be a plurality of *Daseins* that could be *with* one another. In other words, *Dasein* is always a particular; and it is only in the understanding it has of itself that its individuated character has, as it were, been suspended in favor of the "One" to whom all knowledge and choice are attributed.

schuldig.[14] Here, too, a questionable translation of this word as meaning "guilty" has tended to block understanding of Heidegger's meaning. "Guilty" is, indeed, what the word most often means; but the noun *Schuld* also means a "debt" – something owed. There is a way of reconciling these two senses of the term if we assume that we chronically fail to pay this debt and are thus always in arrears. (It is clear that neither one of these notions is to be taken literally or in what Heidegger calls an ontic sense; both are metaphors that have to be explicated in language appropriate to the ontology of human beings.) This assumption actually fits in well with the way Heidegger uses the concept of *Schuld* in this context. By virtue of being the kind of entity we are, we do constitutionally owe something – something is due from each of us – and what is due from each of us is a choice. We are in arrears because we begin in and cannot help preferring the safe anonymity of *Das Man*, which, as Heidegger says, relieves us of the necessity to choose. A choice is due from each of us because there is nothing – neither a God nor any other supra-individual entity or, it might be added, any deterministic theory of our own natures – that can do the work of choice for us by providing the maxim or goal for our actions that would guarantee their justifiability.

This is a fact that we chronically try to hide from ourselves; but it is also possible to accept it or, as Heidegger puts it, to choose choice as the governing modality of one's active life.[15] When we do that, we may be said to "want to have a conscience" in the sense of being prepared to supply, out of one's own resources, what is not in any case forthcoming from any other source. It is this willingness that constitutes authentic responsibility; and the stance in life that it brings into being is what Heidegger calls "resoluteness" (*Entschlossenheit*). In effect, this is his version of autonomous moral agency; but this autonomy is conceived in isolation from anything like the moral law that was its essential counterpart in Kant's ethical theory.

In these circumstances, the question inevitably arises as to whether this choice that we are called to make is itself subject to any standard of judgment. In other words, in choosing authentically can we fail or go wrong in some sense that has ethical relevance or does resoluteness itself constitute the only warrant we can have for what we do? It does not appear that an answer to this question (and certainly not an affirmative one) can be gathered from Heidegger's writings. It is surely significant, however, that the account he gives of conscience makes no mention of other human beings as figuring somehow in this responsibility that is constitutionally ours. It is true that what he says about conscience (and especially about the self-respect that

---

14 Heidegger appears to think that a complete break with *Das Man* is not possible. For a suggestion of the sense in which this thesis might prove to be true, see Chapter 1, section IV.

15 The idea of choosing choice is invoked in *Being and Time*, pp. 312 and 314.

heeding its call generates) applies to all of us. By itself, however, this does not ensure that there will be a reciprocal acknowledgment of an equivalence between one human being and another on the basis of their wanting-to-have-a-conscience or that any such acknowledgment will be an integral element within resoluteness.[16] Unfortunately, this leaves us without an explanation of how Heidegger can say that "we are for the sake of others." As long as this is the case, we are not in a position to show that the *Mitsein* to which this *Fürsorge* is so central has a bearing on the ethical substance of what we do in the mode of authentic choice or resoluteness in which we accept responsibility for our own actions.

One explanation of Heidegger's failure to formulate or answer these questions may be that he regarded choices between moral alternatives as an ontic matter and not properly an ontological one at all and that a discussion of such ontic matters would have been out of place in a book devoted to ontological questions. This distinction appears to be mainly a contrast between the business of life that we discharge without any explicit appeal to the distinctive character of our own being and the kind that is informed by just such an understanding. The difficulty about this is that Heidegger says that we have a pre-ontological understanding of just the matters that are expressly formulated in the language of ontology.[17] It cannot be the case, therefore, that the ontic elements in human life are to be flatly contrasted with everything ontological. To draw just one inference from this fact, it would follow that when we make a choice that affects other people, we do so with a certain understanding of the *Mitsein* we share with them; and this *Mitsein* is an *existentiale,* a constituent element in our ontological constitution. But if *Mitsein* entails, as Heidegger has told us it does, "our being for the sake of others," how could we deny all ontological import to questions that arise in the context of our relations with others? If we were to do so, it would follow that the status of *Mitsein* itself can be ontological only in some sense that excludes any ethical character that may be implicit in the relation to others it constitutes. That, in turn, would mean that our being for the sake of others would have no status within *Mitsein* that is privileged over, say, not caring one way or another about these same others. But

16 The closest Heidegger comes to saying anything like this is his statement that resoluteness "pushes (the self) into solicitous being with others" (*Being and Time,* p. 344).

It is worth noting that in *Grundprobleme der Phänomenologie, Abteilung* II, vol. 24 of the *Gesamtausgabe,* p. 192, Heidegger gives an account of Kant's conception of the *Würde* (moral worth) that accrues to anyone who subordinates his will to the moral law. As often happens, Heidegger uses his own philosophical language to express Kant's point; and this suggests at the least that that point is not uncongenial to his own way of thinking. Interestingly, however, when he says, for example, that respect for the moral law is nothing other than being responsible to oneself and for oneself, nothing is said about respect for the other human being whose interests may be implicated in the matter that is brought under the moral law.

17 See *Being and Time,* p. 35.

any such conclusion would go too directly against Heidegger's own words to be acceptable.

This is the point, then, at which an amplification of Heidegger's account of *Mitsein* seems to be required if it is not to prove ethically vacuous. What such an amplification must accomplish is to show how the choices human beings make can be subject to an ethical constraint from which we cannot release ourselves simply by choosing to do so. It is very clear that none of the classic philosophical accounts of the nature of this constraint are acceptable to Heidegger. The reason is that they invariably lapse into an ontological mode that is inappropriate to the kind of entity a human being is. It is inappropriate because it simply postulates that there is a model – an archetype – of some kind to which our actions are to conform. As it is typically understood, this model has a distinctly thinglike or *vorhanden* character.[18] Since human being, by contrast, is grounded in possibility and transcendence, it is always already out beyond any such model or archetype and dealing with questions to which it cannot supply answers. More concretely, when universal validity is claimed for the ethical truths comprised in this archetype and these are supposed to generate directives for conduct in actual situations in which we have to act, ethical conduct under such a norm is being conceived as a matter of repeating the same action in the same circumstances. But it is just the character of this repetition (*Wiederholung*) that turns out to be less straightforward than we imagine it to be.[19]

This is what Gadamer has shown in one of the few significant amplifications of Heidegger's thought.[20] What he has shown is that since universal prescriptions are not self-interpreting for the full range of situations to

18 The notion of the *vorhanden* is that of something that can be disclosed independently of any context of meaning to which it may otherwise belong. In this respect, it is rather like the notion of extensionality in analytical philosophy. In this case, of course, it is a rule rather than an object of some kind that is being so described, but the point Heidegger is making is still valid. That is that although this rule is supposed to be something that can be fully understood simply in the form of words that is used to express it, it actually refers beyond itself to a wide range of situations that are occasions for choice and action and it implicitly claims to decide these "cases" in advance. But the idea that one can settle things in this formulaic way really amounts to an avoidance of real choice in an actual situation that may have features not taken into account in the rule.

19 Heidegger argues in *Being and Time*, p. 443, that the whole idea of rule-following as straightforward repeating of the action the rule calls for is really a relapse into *das Man*. Real repetition (*Wiederholung*), in Heidegger's sense, is always a more complex affair that involves a response to "the possibility of the existence that has been there" (p. 438). In this sense, while *Dasein* chooses among possibilities in terms of "the mode of interpretation that has come down to us," it does so in a way that involves its being "against [it] and again for [it]" (p. 435). In other words, even its acceptance of what has come down to it involves adaptations and modifications so that what it is finally "for" is never quite the same as what was originally proposed to it.

20 Hans-Georg Gadamer, *Truth and Method* (New York: Seabury Press, 1975).

which they may have to be applied and have to be carried forward into cases that may differ from their predecessors in ways that could not be foreseen when they were originally formulated, their import may become quite ambiguous. In these circumstances, the only effective universality of which such rules are susceptible is one that, as in the case of the common law, emerges gradually from their application to an indefinitely wide range of cases. Because even the most sincere attempt to comply with ethical rules must adapt them to altered circumstances, the idea that our standards of conduct could be reduced to absolutely stable formulas has to be given up. Heidegger insists that the people who are willing to act only under such auspices are really unwilling to accept the responsibility that is entailed by the reconsideration that new circumstances require. Indeed, as he says, any account that reduces action to mechanical rule-following would cancel out the very possibility of acting and reduce the role of the human agent to that of a kind of spectator of his own life.[21] The real issue thus turns out to be how a human agent can be responsive to something that constrains his choices without falling back into an archetype/copy theory of ethical conduct.

It would be interesting to compare this critique of traditional doctrines of ethical truth with Heidegger's treatment of the correspondence theory of truth. The point he makes there is that the alleged correspondence between a thought (or statement) and a state of the world is improperly conceived as a match of some kind between two entities that both have a thinglike character.[22] In other words, the prior disclosure of these terms of comparison has been simply presupposed and no ontological provision has been made for it. Instead of postulating some mysterious match-up between two such terms in this kind of abstraction from the fact of disclosure, Heidegger elects to identify truth in its primordial sense with disclosure as such and to jettison the whole idea of a correspondence between something in the mind and something outside it.[23] As applied to the case of ethical truths, this would

---

21 *Being and Time,* p. 340. What this clearly implies is that under the regime of *Das Man* the only action one is capable of is a pseudo-action because there has been no real choice by the agent.

22 What Heidegger has in mind here is a certain reification of the statement in which some state of the world is expressed. In this reified form, statements are passed around, as it were, from one person to another and generally treated as though their mode of being were that of things rather than that of *Dasein.* When this happens, it is as though they were simply items that, in complete abstraction from the fact of disclosure, could be compared with another such item, namely, the relevant state of the world.

23 Heidegger has sometimes been accused of having simply repudiated the idea of truth as accuracy. It is true that he launched many polemics against truth as *Richtigkeit* (correctness), but the point he was making on those occasions really has to do with the blindness, on the part of the partisans of truth as correspondence, to every other aspect of truth, most especially its character as an uncovering of the entities about which truth is sought. It does not follow from this that Heidegger was simply indifferent to the "getting it right" side of truth.

suggest that, instead of a match-up between an archetype that defines right conduct and our judgments and actions, anything that deserves to be called an ethical truth must itself be a form of disclosure in which something that is not simply *vorhanden* shows itself to be such that it constitutes a limit on the choices we can make.

III

The only case in which this seems possible is one in which the entity that is disclosed is of the same kind as the entity that discloses it – that is, something whose mode of being is ek-sistence – and this means another human being. There are a great many ways in which one human being can disclose another; but many of these abstract from ek-sistence as the mode of being of a human being and, as a result, are not notably different from disclosures of natural objects.[24] But when one human being recognizes another as an active being that both discloses things in the world and reciprocates the disclosure of which it is the object, one can justifiably claim that something has been disclosed that is radically different from anything thinglike or *vorhanden*. An "active being" in this context is one that transcends what is actual in the situation and projects an outcome with which, if it is realized, its fellow human beings will have to live. What emerges in the disclosure of such an agent by his fellow human beings is thus a fact of the same order as their own actions; and if it is such that it blocks or frustrates those actions, it sets up a conflict and implicitly poses a question about what is to be done to resolve it. In the nature of the case, that question has to be understood as being addressed to both parties to this conflict. As long as they simply persist in their respective courses of action, there will eventually be a collision and the matter will have to be settled by force. What this question asks is thus whether there is anything in this situation with its dual reciprocating disclosure of two like entities that establishes a responsibility for them to resolve the issue between them in some other way.

The simple and traditional answer to this question would have been that there is indeed something of this kind: a rule or a moral truth that tells us which one of the two conflicting actions is the right one. Since that answer has already been shown to be unacceptable to Heidegger, we have to ask if there is anything in his thought that does have a bearing on this issue. In his account of conscience he invokes a conception of responsibility that derives

---

24 It is sometimes thought that because Heidegger says so little about the human body, it must fall outside the ontological analysis he presents of human being. This cannot be the case since that would mean that a human being is half *vorhanden* and half ek-sistent; and there is nothing in Heidegger's writings to support such an absurd view. The only consistent interpretation is to treat ek-sistence as the mode of being of the body as it is of the human being as a whole. I have sketched a defense of such a view in *What Is a Human Being?*, ch. 6.

from the unavoidability for each of us of making a response to the situations we are in by taking some action. (This action may, of course, take the form of inaction and thus of letting something happen that we could have tried to prevent.) In the account Heidegger gives of it, the responsibility that is generated in such situations appears to be a matter of acknowledging to oneself that whatever action one takes is one's own action and no one else's. It is a responsibility to choose and it is, by all evidence, a responsibility that is owed in each case to oneself alone as a condition of achieving full authenticity for oneself as a human being.

The difficulty about this is that responsibility normally involves both someone to whom one is responsible and something for which one is responsible; and Heidegger's version of responsibility appears to be problematic in both these respects. For one thing, when we are responsible to ourselves alone, it seems that we could simply release ourselves from that responsibility; and yet this is surely not what Heidegger has in mind. Even if we make no difficulty about this, however, we can hardly suppose that just any random choice would realize a fully authentic form of selfhood as well as any other would. But if only a choice that is significant and consequential within some life can express the kind of responsibility Heidegger has in mind, then it is almost certain to be one that engages the interests of others as well as one's own. Nevertheless, Heidegger does not say that this responsibility would also be a responsibility *to* anyone else. As has been pointed out, he does say that we can (try to) help others to acknowledge their own being as care (*Sorge*), but he does not connect this with the notion of responsibility and certainly not of responsibility to anyone else.

The question this raises is whether it would be possible for one human being to "have a conscience" and thus be responsible in the special sense Heidegger gives this notion without taking into consideration anything except his own preferences in the choices he makes. Given the fact of *Mitsein*, none of us can claim to be simply ignorant of or oblivious to the fact that things "matter" to others just as they do to us although they may care about different things. To leave others and their needs out of the account in the choices we make would thus require either a pretense that we are not effectively making a choice for them as well as for ourselves or an attempt to justify the different weight that is given to one's own preferences over theirs by showing that the action in question serves their interest as well as ours. Broadly speaking, the latter alternative represents the only way people can live together otherwise than by coercion. By some means or other (and these can be very different from explicit argument) they must persuade one another that something like this is the case. If there is any truth claim that is implicit in social and thus in moral life, this is it.[25] By contrast, the first alternative

25 There are obviously a great many considerations that have a bearing on the beneficial character of an action that cannot be noticed here. The difference between short-range and

amounts to a denial of the *Mitsein* that is the premise of Heidegger's whole argument. (That is, effectively, what Sartre does when he insists that, in our relation to them, other human beings are unavoidably reduced to the status of things.) But in the latter case, we would be accepting the responsibility that is implicit in any effort to justify what one does to someone else.

To summarize, unless a fully authentic choice could have any content at all, it will unavoidably express the interests, however construed, of the human being who makes it. These interests, in turn, will stand in some relation to the interests of others; and any meaningful form of responsibility will have to take those into account. This means that a responsible person must offer some reason to himself and to these same others for the priority that has been assigned to his own interests over theirs, if that is what his choice involves. My being responsible thus means that my choice must be such that it can be presented as being at least compatible with some wider form of life in which there is a place for others that is arguably consistent with their interests. But at the same time, each of us must understand that the people to whom this justification is offered are in principle capable of determining whether the claim it makes – namely, that their interest is served by the action in question – is true or not.

The only alternative to this choice between an attempt to reify others that must fail and an effort to justify what one does to them is force. Regrettably, there are not a few signs that Heidegger may have inclined toward a Nietzschean conception of the contrast between those who can take ultimate responsibility for their lives and those who cannot.[26] That view in effect disqualifies the mass of mankind for anything like moral partnership. When it is adopted, there is a strong temptation to conceive the role of the "strong" who *are* capable of being responsible as that of masters who drive the common herd before them. Their spiritual superiority is supposed to justify this coercion as it does the dismissal of the interests of those lesser beings as irrelevant to any determination of the responsibilities of their masters since these are held to be of an altogether higher spiritual order. But if assumptions of this kind are not made, responsibility will have to be construed in terms like those set forth above; and it will have to be accepted that there is no absolute contrast between those who can judge whether something is fair to all concerned and those who cannot. We all know, of course, that there

---

long-range benefits is one such; and another would be the fact that long-run benefits can often be produced by authorizing people to act in ways that will undoubtedly cause harm to others although with the prospect of eventual gain. This kind of freedom is what distinguishes a competitive market economy, in which in the short run a lot of people may get hurt, but which ultimately benefits many by the release of productive forces that this freedom is supposed to effect. The great and still unresolved issue about this freedom is whether its benefits really do accrue to everyone.

26 See, for example, the contrast Heidegger makes between the *Volk* and *die eigentlich Schaffenden* – those who really create – in *Holderlins Hymnen "Germanien" und "Der Rhein,"* *Gesamtausgabe*, Abteilung II, vol. 39, p. 51.

are great differences among human beings in this respect. To exploit those, however, for the purpose either of gaining an unfair advantage or of disqualifying some people entirely from participation in such decisions is itself a tactic that cannot possibly be justified to the people whom it would affect.

It is worth noting that the kind of responsibility I am describing is already implicit in the relationship in which we stand to other human beings simply at the level of the co-disclosure of things in our common world. If I notice something and say to my co-discloser that it is a such-and-such, he may well draw my attention to some feature of this object that is inconsistent with its being a such-and-such. If I am to adhere to my original identification, I must then come back with some consideration that shows that the feature in question is not what my colleague takes it to be or that even if it is, the object in question can still be what I took it to be. (I might, of course, simply concede that he is right and I am wrong about this.) However we understand *Mitsein,* it must comprise a capability for engaging in exchanges of this kind; and to the extent that we do so engage, we will be concerned to produce an understanding of what is the case that both of us (and anyone else who may happen along) can share. In this sense, our vis-à-vis in *Mitsein* and we ourselves must be familiar with the business of arriving at a disclosure that is as close as possible to being genuinely common and neutral as between the persons concerned.

When we turn from observation to issues of action and choice, it may seem that everything must be quite different because there is, *ex hypothesi,* no independent prior fact – no truth – out there that both of us are trying to establish. To suppose that, in contexts of choice, there is such a fact would be just the kind of category mistake that throws us into the arms of *Das Man.* The concept of truth has played a notably equivocal role in the history of ethical theory if only because when it is invoked, we tend to construe it in terms of familiar paradigms of factual truth and assume that it functions in the same way in the one context and the other. But even if we accept all this and acknowledge that there is, crudely put, nothing out there that tells us what we must do, this does not mean that the concept of truth has no bearing on matters involving ethical choice. The reason is that the partnership with other human beings established by our symmetrical relation to what is the case in the world remains in being even after this acknowledgment. And since this is a partnership in which the truth that both parties seek has its place within active undertakings on the part of the one and the other of these persons, it is natural that the wider shared understandings that govern the search for the truth should be extended to the resolution of conflicts in the area of action.

The parallelism between these two kinds of situations can be made even more concrete. Since Heidegger speaks of choice and action as being themselves disclosive in nature and as disclosing possibilities, there is a persuasive analogy here between the disclosure of things in the world – the kind that is supposed to be "neutral" and "objective" – and the disclosure of possibilities that are in effect so many different modes of *Mitsein*. But the basis of the analogy is not the fact that a question of truth can arise in connection with possibilities as it does with actualities – namely, in the form of the question, Is this *really* possible? That is indeed the case; but the more important question raised by possibilities when they can be realized by some action is whether they are desirable or not. About that everyone can have an opinion because anyone may be affected by the action that realizes the possibility; and everyone can ask why one possibility is to be preferred to another. It follows that the primary requirement that a possible action must satisfy is one that has to do with the good it would bring about; and since there may be many human beings who are affected by that action, the good (or its opposite) it realizes must be acceptable in principle to them or preferable to any other action that might be possible in the given circumstances.

When we are trying to determine what is the case, that is, true, the outcome of such an inquiry must be the same for everyone. When it is a possible action that is under consideration, the consequences of that action will differ widely from one person to another. But if it can be shown to be preferable to any other in terms of the way it affects people's lives, then there is a sense in which these consequences will be the same for all; and in that respect it will be like truth. There is, in other words, a more general condition of acceptability to an open class of persons that is implicit in *Mitsein* and that encompasses both truth in the familiar sense and the rightness of an action that satisfies the requirement just described. In this sense, our *Mitsein* commits us, in the field of action, to an attitude toward others that is in its essentials comparable to that toward our partners in the search for truth. Any other attitude would separate the two elements in our lives referred to above in a way that amounts to a denial of our *Mitsein* by repudiating the complementarity of disclosure in its full amplitude; and it would thereby remove any motive we might otherwise have for collaboration in the determination of the truth.

What I am proposing, then, is that although there is no antecedent truth about what we are to do, truth understood as constituting a complementarity of disclosure among human beings becomes the model for the complementarity to one another of our choices and actions and those of other human beings.[27] What makes this a valid parallelism is the fact that we are dealing with beings – other human beings – whose relation to what is the case as well as to what might be the case is in principle the same as ours. If

27 I believe an idea of this kind has been proposed by Hector-Neri Castañeda but in a very different philosophical context. I am familiar only with a passing reference to it in a paper of his that I saw a good many years ago but have not been able to trace.

I have the kind of responsibility to them that was described above, that can be met only by pointing to something actual and/or possible that counts for them, for purposes of justification, in the same way as it counts for me when a certain action is under consideration. In this sense, just as, in the case of things in the world, what I disclose must be compatible with what other people disclose and is ideally complementary to it, so in the domain of action I can be responsible only if I can show that the action I propose to take stands in some compatible/complementary relation to the actions of others who may be affected by it, provided their actions satisfy the same criterion.

In Chapter 1 it was argued that another human being is quite literally an Alter Ego as well as simply an Alter. This identity in difference is due to the fact that, for all the great differences that set one human being apart from others, any human being as an entity that has a world is the same as any other because that world is the same for every human being. We may have wildly different "beliefs" about the world and it may be impossible in practice to resolve these differences; and yet this is not enough to make us give up the idea of a single world that is, in principle, the same for all. But if our human being is understood in terms of that common truth for which we collectively constitute a public forum, it is also the case that everything I can cite in justification of some action must be accessible to those to whom this justification is offered as it is to me. In this sense, I am (or at least I can be) on both sides of any situation in which a conflict arises with another human being; and this holds for matters of choice and action just as it does for matters of belief. Accordingly, if the justification I offer for my action is that it serves the general good, I am in a position to understand, in a given case, the falsity of that claim in light of the consequences my action may have for someone else. Most important of all, I cannot simply disallow the claim that emanates from that person because it is all too likely to be the claim I would make in those circumstances myself. If, nevertheless, I simply brush aside the testimony of those who oppose my action, I will unavoidably be at odds with myself and the truth or validity that I claim for the case I make for my action will be exposed at the same time as a lie in my own eyes.[28]

28 It might be objected to the line of thought I have been developing that what has just been described is really just a language game with its own rules and that the only conclusion one can draw really just comes down to this, namely, that anyone who accepts the opening gambit in this game can hardly decline to accept the outcome that those rules dictate. The deflationary effect of comments like this is due to the fact that they make it sound as though an ethical conclusion – "X has acted wrongly" – were itself somehow just a move in a language game and as such somehow detached from any realities in the field of conduct. It seems likely that both those who offer such observations and those who respond to them in this way are under the influence of certain stereotypical expectations as to what an ethical fact would have to look like and that it is these expectations that make it seem as though something that has turned out to be the outcome of a language game can hardly count as the momentous kind of thing an ethical fact is supposed to be. If that is the case, then it

This line of thought can be taken further by linking Heidegger's concept of *Mitsein* with the Hegelian notion of recognition.[29] In our ordinary way of thinking about such matters, there is nothing especially difficult about recognizing another human being. Familiar criteria such as the configuration of the body and the capacity for speech are usually quite adequate to the task of making such identifications. The trouble with this short way with the matter is that it identifies human beings by the way they figure within the perspective of an external observer and thus treats them as objects of a certain kind that turn up in the latter's world. In Hegel's dialectic of the master and the slave in his *Phenomenology of Spirit*, by contrast, recognition of someone as being, like oneself, a human being is shown to be anything but this kind of unproblematic ascertaining of an empirical fact. What is at issue in that dialectic is precisely whether the self and the other are in fact the same in the relevant sense of complementing one another. At issue, therefore, is the relation in which the will – the choices and actions – of one person is to stand to that of another: who is to command and who is to obey? But this turns out to be a question that I cannot simply settle one way or another by myself. This is because we cannot evade the fact of the presence of another being like ourselves who has his own answer to that question and to whom our answer must be given. This fact is the fact of *Mitsein*, and it is an ethical fact because our response to it is given not so much by what we say as by the way we act – that is, by whether we acknowledge our vis-à-vis as sharing the kind of identity we claim for ourselves. In Hegel's view, that is what is ultimately at stake when we have to determine whether we are to grant recognition to another human being.

As we all know, there are plenty of reasons for refusing recognition to others as being our equals in this vital respect. If we can coerce others or deceive them in such a way as to blind them to the truth about their own

may be time for us to consider the possibility that these expectations are leading us to miss the ethical "facts" of a given situation because we are looking for them in the wrong places and do not recognize the real thing when it turns up. This in turn suggests the possibility that, if we hang on to these preconceptions, we are not really very interested in conceiving these facts in a way that would give us a real prospect of finding any. The right place is the world as a space that is inhabited by human beings who are with one another although not simply in the side-by-side manner that expresses a mutual externality; whose *Mitsein* impinges on the things that matter to them; and who finally have to be able to count on one another if they are to have any hope of achieving any real control over the world they are in. And if that is the right place, then an ethical fact is one that emerges at the conclusion of the kinds of exchanges between Ego and Alter I have been discussing. The common feature of such conclusions is that they show something to be wrong because it implicitly denies an identity between Ego and Alter that the agent is not in a position to repudiate because he has to count on it for so many purposes of his own.

29 The principal source for the account I give here of Hegel's conception of recognition is his *Phenomenology of Spirit*, translated by A. V. Miller (Oxford: Oxford University Press, 1977). The section on Self-Consciousness is of special importance.

interests, conspicuous advantages often accrue to us as a result of our establishing ourselves as the masters. This can make it seem that the denial of an equivalence between two individuals or groups that may be obvious to others is simply a fraud in the service of greed. The point I am making, however, is that it is a conflict not just between one will – one self-interest – and another but between two typically egocentric versions of the relation in which these parties stand to one another and thus of the equivalence/ nonequivalence of the self and the other. In this sense, it is the constitution of a moral community that is at issue on these occasions; and it is that aspect of the ethical life to which the concept of *Mitsein* is primarily relevant. Such a community can be formed only if both sides can reach a single version of the truth about who they are and can also in that sense accept the equivalence of the one and the other in their understanding of that truth.[30] In Hegel's account, this conflict and its resolution are embedded in a process that is guaranteed to culminate in an understanding – itself part of the process – that defines the full meaning of the humanity that appears at different stages within it, as in these examples, only in distorted or fragmentary forms. Such a framework is not available for Heidegger or for this inquiry.

There is at least one feature of Hegel's wider conception that can be appropriated, however, and that is the idea of an internal relatedness among the human beings that stand in these reciprocal relationships of recognizing and being recognized. More specifically, this means that to recognize someone as a human being is, in any real life context, to see him as being not only the same as ourselves in the relevant respects but also as someone in whose disclosure of the world we ourselves have a place as he does in ours. More concretely, we have a place there as active beings whose purposes stand in some actual or imaginable relation to those of this human being himself. It follows from this that whatever we may have done that affects something that he as an active being has tried or is trying to accomplish is subject to his judgment as it is to ours without any absolute privilege accruing to either side. The place we occupy in another life may be of little significance or it may be of the greatest importance. In either case, in any authentic *Mitsein*

---

30 Any such view as this is in marked contrast with the position put forward by John Rawls in his *Political Liberalism* (New York: Columbia University Press, 1993). He argues that principles of justice do not presuppose that anything of this kind has been realized and can serve in fact as a basis for coexistence among communities that are not at one with one another in these respects. Against this, I would argue that whatever cultural and other differences may separate such communities from one another, there must be, within each of them and expressed in the appropriate cultural idiom, something very like the kind of recognition that I am postulating as the foundation of morality. To this I would add that in some way or other these communities must find a way of understanding people in other cultural communities in some comparable way. Unless they were able to do that, the likelihood that they would adopt Rawls's principles simply in a *faute de mieux* sort of way seems very slim. See Rawls's discussion of this distinction in *Political Liberalism*, pp. 48–54.

that rests on more than force there is an element of obligation that can be satisfied only by a good-faith effort to understand what is being done on both sides in its relation to the two sets of interests.

To say this is implicitly to underscore the role that the imagination plays in the moral life as our chief means of understanding what another life is like. There is a long story that could be told (but will not be here) about the cultivation and neglect of this vital power and the effects of the one and the other on our perception of human beings.[31] What I want to emphasize instead is the respect in which what has been said about recognition differs from the model of recognition that applies to objects. We say that something is an apple or an abacus or an asteroid and we tend to assume that this same mode of identification can be readily transferred to human beings. In this familiar picture, the objects being subsumed under some classificatory rubric or other do not talk back and so the person who classifies them does not come into the picture – least of all as the object of a reciprocating recognition. Recognition of a human being, by contrast, is a matter, not just of finding him present in our world but of responding to that presence by the modes of choice and action that acknowledge the equivalence of self and other. I cannot, after all, desire that my own purposes should be frustrated by the actions of others. Accordingly, if I acknowledge someone else as being like me in the respects that count for these purposes, I cannot reconcile this recognition with treating him as though his purposes had no standing in my eyes.

It is, as we all know, possible to withhold that recognition. If it is withheld, however, we are once again in the position of having, in principle, to explain why it is withheld and thereby granting with one hand what we hold back with the other. There is another even more serious incoherence in any such life policy. To the extent that we do withhold recognition, we deny ourselves the possibility of being so recognized by others. This is because we cannot help knowing that we have denied them the kind of status which alone could make them capable, in our own eyes, of according us any recognition that would mean anything to us. It may be possible to coerce or bribe or deceive other people into treating us in the ways we desire; but any meaning this could have for us would be fatally undercut by our own unavoidable knowledge of how we brought this about and – even more unwelcome – of the worthlessness of any recognition given by people to whom we have refused any comparable recognition.

There is good reason to believe that most of us do not formulate these alternatives as starkly as this and that we do not choose among them in any

31 Two books that I have found invaluable for the way they develop this thesis are Northrop Frye, *The Educated Imagination* (Bloomington: Indiana University Press, 1964); and Wayne C. Booth, *Modern Dogma and the Rhetoric of Assent* (Chicago: University of Chicago Press, 1974).

explicit way. Instead, we shift back and forth and even try to combine policies that are really utterly inconsistent. What we are struggling with in all
these maneuvers is the contrast between a private economy of purposes
within which other human beings figure only in terms of the ways in which
they can affect *our* purposes and a genuinely public and mutual ordering of
our common life. This a struggle in which not just individual human beings
but collective entities of all kinds engage; and it constitutes the dialectic of
social existence.[32] Unfortunately, this is just the aspect of *Mitsein* that does
not emerge in Heidegger's account of it, which is still dominated by the idea
of an individual choosing the "hero" in his own soul.

It will have been noticed that in the preceding discussion nothing has
been laid down about what is to count as significantly "mattering" to someone. In other words, I have not espoused any theory of value. That omission
will be partly (but only partly) made up for in the next chapter; and I acknowledge that the development of such a theory would be a necessary condition for a comprehensive moral philosophy. It seems clear, however, that
that task would presuppose a condition of *Mitsein;* and so it is legitimate, I
think, to leave it aside in a study devoted to that prior requirement. In this
connection, I should also note that in speaking as I have of the equality and
equivalence of all human beings who are *with* one another in the sense I
have been assuming, I have not paid any attention to the countless circumstances that differentiate the positions we occupy and the functions we perform in a social order. These, too, are matters that need to be negotiated
among people who recognize one another as moral partners and as equal
in the sense that entails. But when such considerations dominate the whole
field of ethical discussion, there is a danger that they will be taken to constitute the substance of the ethical, and the original and primary recognition on which they must rest will be slighted.

IV

Up to this point I have talked mainly about responsibility as the foundational
concept for ethics. This discussion must now be supplemented by an account of the other term in the ethical relation. Since I am always responsible for something and to someone, that someone will be in the position of
relying on me to do whatever it is that I am responsible for. That reliance on
the responsible party by the one to whom he is responsible is what we call
trust. It is this coupling of responsibility with trust that constitutes the partnership out of which more determinate modes of ethical relatedness and especially the fact of obligation arise. For that reason alone, it deserves more
attention than it usually receives.

32 In *The Dialectic of Action: A Philosophical Interpretation of History and the Humanities* (Chicago:
University of Chicago Press, 1979) I attempted to characterize this process.

I will argue that the authority of the ethical limits within which we live is owed to the fact that a failure to respect them would be a violation of the trust placed in us by the people to whom we are responsible. This is not the view that has traditionally been taken of this matter. Instead, there has been a kind of displacement to other venues of the source of ethical authority; and the effect of this displacement has often been to occlude the kinds of considerations that have just been invoked. Thus, in most human communities, our duties are specified in a code of custom and law whose authority rests on tradition – most notably, traditional religious teachings – as well as on the penalties, formal and informal, that are established for violations of these rules. In these circumstances, each of us has responsibilities as a member of a community; but the responsibilities we have are not owed to one another in any radical sense – that is, in any sense that generates the obligation in question itself. In the past, obedience was often thought to be owed to the ruler, whether of the state or of the family, or to God as the ultimate authority for the rule of the one or the other. At present, something like the democratic system of representative government or majority rule in the creation of laws is more likely to be cited. This certainly comes closer to the idea I favor; but as it is usually expounded, it takes on a rather mechanical and bureaucratic aspect that is alien to the spirit of that idea. What is missing is the sense that our responsibilities are to one another and that the fundamental relation of one human being to another is one in which trust is paired with responsibility. An explication of the distinctive rapport that exists between people who trust one another is thus in order.

Although the concept of trust has not figured very prominently in ethical theory, its relevance to the present discussion is not at all difficult to demonstrate. Already at the level of the complementarity of the disclosure of the world effected by one human being to that effected by another, it is evident that what is so disclosed cannot become a resource in the relevant sense unless there is a disposition to rely upon it on the part of the human being to whom it is made available. Such a relationship can arise only if certain conditions are met. Most notably, all these human beings must have a working understanding of the kind of identity between them that it presupposes; and they must be able to communicate with one another in a way that makes the disclosure effected by one of them available to others. This is something we do constantly and, for the most part, in a completely uncalculating and unquestioning manner. The same can be said of the way we incorporate what we learn from others into our own understanding of the way things are in the world and then rely upon it for purposes of our own.

So fundamental a place does this reliance on the corpus of knowledge that is current in our immediate human environment occupy in our lives that it is safe to say that we have no alternative to it. In this respect, it is not unlike what Santayana called "animal faith." Both define conditions that must be met if anything like ordinary human life is to be possible. There is an important difference between the two, however, since the trust of which I speak is a relation to other human beings as bearers of truth, as it is not in Santayana, and only through them to the reality and stability of the natural world. What this comes to is an implicit acceptance of what we learn from those on whom we rely as being true – that is, the way things actually are in the world. This is the practice of truth-telling; it is at work everywhere in human life understood as a tissue of reciprocal understandings resting on responsibility and trust.

When discourse (*Rede*) is understood as the passing on to one human being of what has been disclosed by another, the truth it expresses may or may not have an ethical valence, but the fidelity to the truth on the part of the speaker – his truthfulness – most certainly does. A truthful person is one who may be mistaken and thus say something that is not true; but he cannot do so with the understanding that what he says is not true. Since those involved in such exchanges have interests that may be affected by the truth or falsity of what they are told, truthfulness is plainly an ethical disposition. It may be defined as the conscientious effort to determine for oneself what is true and to make whatever one imparts to others conform to the same standard one uses for oneself. More generally, by virtue of the disclosive character of human being and the communicative character of the relation between human beings, *Mitsein* as a whole becomes the matrix of a relation of these human beings to one another that centers on truth.

It is regrettable that the sheer familiarity of the rule against lying has imparted to it a kind of "goody-goody" quality that may make us feel that it is intended for children and not for us, engaged as we are in the strenuous work of the world.[33] All kinds of more or less sophistical counterexamples have been proposed to show that a rigid adherence to the requirement of truth-telling can do more harm than good. To cite a notable example, Kant's refusal to allow an exception to this rule even when it could save a life is cited as typical of the kind of wrongheadedness to which such rigidity can lead. Unfortunately, when it is conceded that Kant may have carried things a bit too far, this admission seems to have a kind of Open Sesame effect in which any sense of strict obligation we may have had about truth-telling has to compete against a hundred plausible benefits that happen to require a bit of deception. And yet, boring or not, the absolutely central place of truth-telling in our ethical life can hardly be questioned. A lie is, after all, the necessary first step in all manner of wrongdoing, and it is one that is especially easy to justify to ourselves if we are full of a sense of our own benevolent intentions.

33 For example, when Sissela Bok's *Lying: Moral Choice in Public and Private Life* (New York: Pantheon Books, 1978) was published, it can hardly be said that its reception among the liberal intelligentsia was enthusiastic. See, for example, the review by David Bazelon in *The Times Literary Supplement*, August 11, 1978, p. 907.

Nor is the prohibition against it simply something for small children to inscribe in their copybooks; it is an element in the understandings that undergird our social institutions.

This is notably the case for language as the basis of human sociality and, as such, is a cardinal illustration of the cooperative character of our disclosure of the world. This aspect of language is usually dealt with by philosophers under the rubric of "pragmatics" – a rather makeshift category that is supposed to accommodate any feature of language that does not fit easily into either semantics or syntax. As practiced by most philosophers, pragmatics deals mainly with contextual features of speech acts that are tacitly supplied by the speaker but may affect the meaning and thus the comprehensibility to someone else of what he says. An example would be the presuppositions implicit in some utterance that may not be available to one's interlocutor. More relevantly for the purposes of this inquiry, Jürgen Habermas has developed a theory of pragmatics in which presuppositions of another order are central.[34] These are not the contextual contingencies of discourse that are usually taken up, but the quite general understandings that have to be in place on both sides if any kind of discursive exchange is to have a point. Even more significantly, Habermas is concerned to show that these understandings are pervasively ethical in character and that the relation between people engaging in speech acts is itself an ethical one. He does not, however, invoke for this purpose any special philosophical concept of the human person although the one that has been developed here would seem to have major affinities with his line of thought. Still, this very fact may add a significant increment of authority to the conclusions he draws since their convergence with those reached here was in no way dictated by some prior affinity in matters of philosophical anthropology.

Habermas conceives language use as "communicative action" – action that is designed to bring about the agreement among human beings that is a necessary condition for cooperative work. On this account, there is implicit in such communication a number of "validity claims" in the absence of which any communicative exchange would have no point. The most salient of these is the claim that what the speaker says is true; and this claim is reinforced by an implicit assurance that the speaker is speaking truthfully. This means that even if what he says should turn out to be false, it is something that he in good conscience believed to be true at the time of utterance. What these claims do is commit the speaker to an assurance to his interlocutor by the terms of which any attempt to differentiate between what he tells his interlocutor and what he himself is prepared to rely upon is ruled out. Unless it were understood on both sides that these validity claims form part of what

---

34 See Habermas's essay, "What Is Universal Pragmatics?" in *Communication and the Evolution of Society,* translated by Thomas McCarthy (Boston: Beacon Press, 1979).

the speaker is conveying to his vis-à-vis, the latter could have no rational motive for listening to what he says. In other words, it is the mutuality thus realized in the communicative relation that constitutes its ethical character.

Suppose, for example, that I were to ask a factual question of someone and that person were to answer my question by telling me that something or other is the case. I might then proceed to act in some way or other on the basis of what he has told me and my action might well succeed or fail depending on the truth or falsity of that answer. It seems plain that in these circumstances the person who gave the answer will be at least partly responsible for the outcome. Not only that, but this fact itself is something that he has to understand. He has implicitly authorized his interlocutor to treat his answer as expressing what he believes to be the case; and so there is no way he can appeal to a contrast between his answer – his saying that such and such is the case – and what *he* believes. That would pervert the sense of the exchange that took place between these two people. That sense is defined by the understanding the questioner has of what he is doing as much as it is by that of the one who answers. What is vital to the whole transaction is that that sense be the same for both of them.

There can, of course, be no absolute guarantee that the vicarious disclosure that *Mitsein* affords us will in fact be trustworthy. As I will show in the next chapter, one could even say that our depending on others for information creates an opportunity for abuse that would not otherwise exist. But in spite of all the worldly-wise cynicism that the experience of such abuse can inspire, there really is no general alternative to the reliance on others that makes it possible. We can, of course, devise sensible criteria for determining when what someone tells us is likely to be less than reliable and when it may even be deceitful. What I am suggesting, however, is that these are criteria that in one way or another qualify a massive prior trust in other human beings upon which the communicative function of language and thus language itself depend. Accordingly, it would not be possible to generalize the *dis*trust implicit in the use of such criteria and to require that there always be good reasons to accept what someone says and not just that there be no reasons not to accept it. In this sense, language as the fundamental institution that makes society possible among human beings presupposes and is itself based on trust among those who participate in language-mediated social practices. This is a trust that is predicated on the assumed truthfulness of the person whose statement we accept and thus on the assumed truth of what he tells us.

Up to this point I have been discussing a kind of trust among human beings that is largely implicit and inarticulate, although we may try to formalize it in various ways. The ethical relation this involves is not, it should be noticed, an obligation to supply whatever information we need on demand, but rather not to lie. Plainly, that obligation derives from a more general one that is not necessarily or principally discursive in nature – the obligation not to do harm to others. There are other modalities of the ethical relation that involve both responsibility and trust and that require more of us than that. What is required is help – one form or another of assistance that enables us to achieve something or to avoid some bad outcome that would otherwise occur. There are situations in which there can be an obligation, not just to avoid harm but to render aid. These are sometimes called natural obligations; and they express a kind of minimum level of concern for others – whether they live or die, for example, in circumstances in which rescue is possible without undue risk to oneself. It is very doubtful whether people who were not prepared to come to one another's assistance in such circumstances could be moral partners in any other respect. But the more common case is the one in which we ask for such assistance and someone agrees to provide it. To do that is to make a promise, and our reliance on such promises is another major form that trust assumes.

Promises are typically asked for and given in situations in which it is not just information that is needed – one cannot, in any case, *promise* that something is the case – but some action by the promisor that has a special importance for the promisee. Even if I trust the person in question, the fact that this trust *can* be violated is enough to make us want some stronger and more formal assurance. Someone may say that he intends to do what I in fact want him to do; but he can do that while retaining complete freedom to change his mind. What is needed is that in full recognition of my hope and expectation he should bind himself to the performance of what he has said he will do so that I can rely on that performance with perfect confidence. In archaic societies the words used to effect this binding often had a magical aura about them that, it was thought, would somehow compel the parties to the transaction to do their part. This doubtless explains, for example, the fanatical insistence of the Romans on absolute fidelity to the exact words prescribed in such formulas as a necessary condition for their binding force.[35]

Promise-making as we understand it now is a rather anemic descendant of these practices; but like them it is intended to formalize an understanding and to do so in a way that, to the degree possible, removes any element of optionality that it might otherwise be thought to contain. In our own day, promising has received a good deal of attention within moral philosophy; and in social contract theories it has even been proposed as what establishes a political society and the civil relation to one another of its members. Even without making such large claims for it, it is evident that promising does modify the relation between the people who are parties to it. To promise is

---

35 On this point, see Axel Hägestrom, *Inquiries into the Nature of Law and Morals,* edited by K. Olivekrona (Stockholm: Almkvist and Wiksell, 1953).

to assure someone that we will act (or not act) in a certain way on some occasion or in some defined set of circumstances. This assurance is not just a statement of fact concerning my future actions; it is an authorization given to the person to whom the promise is made to base his own plans on the expectation that what is being promised will be done. It may be that certain conditions are implicit (and perhaps even explicit) in the utterance by which the promise is made and that these are such as to excuse nonperformance in certain circumstances. There is one condition, however, that a promise cannot contain; it cannot be a promise to do or not do something "if I feel like it." In other words, the promise-maker denies himself in advance the right he might otherwise have to make something depend solely on his own preferences at the time. In so doing, he implicitly accepts that a failure to perform when no excusing condition holds will put him in the wrong and also that his being or not being in the wrong is not something that he alone has the power to determine. In this respect, promising is like the search for the truth in that it removes something from the area of my life over which I have plenary powers and acknowledges that at least for these purposes there is someone else who has the same rights that I claim for myself when it comes to determining what is required.

It would be wrong to suppose that all promises are made in a fully explicit or formulaic manner or that responsibility and trust are in order only when they are. The trust of a small child in its parents was never authorized in any such way and yet the responsibility to which it corresponds is just as authentic as it would be if *per impossibile* it had been. In such cases it is clear that having a child is by itself the assumption of such a responsibility and that the trust in its parents that a child feels is the natural response to the care and love they give it.[36] Again, we do not promise one another that we will not steal from or otherwise harm one another, but here again such an understanding is implicit in any common life since it is a necessary condition for any wider form of cooperation. In many communities – usually small ones – people trust one another not to do these things and feel a corresponding responsibility not to do them themselves. This trust is evident in the fact that they do not lock their doors and they take walks alone at night. Unhappily, in larger cities where most of us are unknown to one another, that kind of trust is typically eroded to the point where we make our homes fortresses from which we go forth only with great caution.

What has just been said shows that there is a significant affinity between truth-telling and promising. Although a promise is not usually described as being true (or false) in the way that a factual statement is, it would not be difficult to work out a sense in which these predicates could be appropri-

---

36 On the duties of parents, see my "Rights and Duties in Education," in *Educational Judgments*, edited by James F. Doyle (London: Routledge and Kegan Paul, 1973).

ately applied to promises. When I promise someone that I will do something, I am not *predicting* that I will do x, since that would mean that I would only need to stand by and see what happens. (If I did anything but watch, I could in fact be accused of "cooking the data.") But keeping a promise is precisely doing something to insure a certain outcome. Even though a promise is not a prediction, whether a promise is kept or not depends on whether it is true that I do x at the appropriate time. In the case of a promise, there can be no question of simply waiting to see what happens as we do in the case of a prediction. Instead, I as the promisor have to *make* it the case. What differentiates a promise from a prediction is the fact that the words I use, "I will do x," have an indeterminate truth-value if only because the time of performance has not yet come. When it does, not doing x without any plausible explanation of why I could not do it amounts to a violation of the undertaking I gave; and it must be wrong in my own eyes as well as in those of the person whom I misled.

This discussion of truth-telling and promising has shown both to have a structure that in its essentials is the same. Both are practices that are possible only because those who participate in them share a common understanding of what is required of them and thus of what they cannot do without having to recognize that they are in the wrong vis-à-vis the other participant(s). In both cases the binding character of the relation between these people is self-imposed and is a condition for whatever benefits are expected to flow from that relation. So fundamental are the relations among human beings defined by these practices that it is impossible to imagine any form of social life in which they would not have a place. It is possible, however, to take part in these practices without really complying with their requirements and even without ever intending to. Because of that fact, both kinds of relation rest ultimately on trust – the willingness to allow something of value to oneself to depend on the compliance of another person with the understandings that are in place between the two (or more) parties to some undertaking.

To this account of responsibility and trust, it should be added that each of us is, on different occasions and in different contexts, both the responsible party and the one who trusts. If anything, this fact should intensify our sense of being on both sides of such understandings and, consequently, of the stringency of the obligation they involve, even when our deepest desires may come into conflict with that obligation. This presumption is doubtless broadly correct; but it would not do to underestimate the ingenuity with which we and our fellow humans seek to have things our way while still maintaining a color of legitimacy for what we in fact wind up doing. The next chapter will deal with that aspect of our moral experience as well as others that are akin to it.

It is obvious that there are a great many issues raised by this discussion of trust that cannot be dealt with here. Notable among them is the difficulty raised by relationships of trust that are in conflict with one another. Yet another is the question whether the notion of trust itself is not tied to personal relationships and whether it can really be transferred intact to the sphere of the public and collective business of mankind. By way of an anticipatory answer to questions such as these, the following observation must do duty for a fuller account. If trust is the central modality of *Mitsein* and if this is the sense we give to Heidegger's somewhat cryptic thesis that by virtue of this *Mitsein* we are *umwillen Anderer* – for the sake of others – then it must follow that trust cannot be confined to one part of our relations to others. It must be the form of our *Mitsein* as a whole. There can be no real trust among people who reserve the right to act on some other occasion or in some other matter in a way that does not even pretend to honor the kind of identity between Ego and Alter that I have been postulating. This suggests a further point. To live with one another on the basis of a sense of trust always leads us to expect that that trust, however ill-defined, will hold for an indefinite range of situations that may have yet to arise. If in such circumstances someone were to reclaim an unrestricted freedom of action in some new situation not covered by existing understandings, he would typically catch his partners unprepared, and if so, he would have gained the advantage by exploiting the trust built up by cooperative practices for the purpose of achieving some selfish end that does not include them. In such cases, it is clear that the prior existence of relationships of trust is a necessary condition for the realization of purposes that are themselves unshareable and that in this sense evil is parasitical upon good. This is a theme that will be developed further in the next chapter.

3

EVIL AND GOOD

I

The account that has been given of the relationships that derive from *Mitsein* may have made it sound as though they ensured a level of harmony and mutual respect of which, unfortunately, human history shows little trace. If that has happened, this chapter should put things in a more realistic perspective. *Mitsein*, after all, is not, in the first instance, an ideal; it is an ontological condition – what Heidegger calls an existentiale – and as such its reality cannot simply be abrogated by a violation of whatever normative requirements may turn out to be implicit in it. To put it in a different way, *Mitsein* is not just the form of our lives insofar as they conform to some ethical standard; it is a necessary condition for wrongdoing and evil as well.

This means that the concept of Mitsein must be shown to enable us to give an account of these negative realities of the moral life. The basis for such an account has already been laid. What is fundamentally unjustifiable and therefore wrong is to deny our distinctively human commonality with one another by treating someone as though he or she were not a partner in *Mitsein* and had no claim to any consideration in decisions we make about how to act. But even when *Mitsein* and its implications are acknowledged and obligations are accepted, there is always the possibility of a default; and it has been made clear that, barring special circumstances that are relevant to the case in hand, a failure to do one's part in the relationship that gives rise to such an obligation puts the person who so fails in the wrong.

What I will be concerned with in this chapter is not so much a further elaboration of this story, but a deeper systemic flaw that can develop within the scheme of ethical relationships that has been outlined in the preceding chapters. This flaw takes the form of what the Greeks called *stasis* – a notion that might be freely rendered into English as a kind of standoff among the self-interested individuals that make up a human group.[1] I will argue that when self-interest alone, even broadly construed, defines the expectations that each of us brings to our common life, the acknowledgments of one another that derive from our *Mitsein* may not be enough to avoid the kind of deadlock or stalemate in our relationships with one another for which I have chosen to use the word *stasis*. At the same time, I want to show that there is another development of which *Mitsein* is susceptible – one that moves in a quite different direction from the one just noted and in some sense compensates for it in the way that supererogation may be said to compensate for ethical deficiencies elsewhere. In order to develop this idea properly, a brief excursus into ethical theory will be necessary.

There has long been a conflict in our thinking about our social natures that centers on the question of whether justice or love should ultimately govern our relationships with one another. Up to this point, what has been said about *Mitsein* has probably sounded as though it were leaning more to the side of justice than to that of love, but love has a vital role to play here as well; and I will give an account of it in the second part of this chapter. I will argue that this potentiality of *Mitsein* can best be approached through a reconsideration of the contrast between the good and the right. More specifically, the argument I will make in this chapter is designed to show that the good and the right are more closely associated than they are usually thought to be. This revision of the contrast between the two will also be associated with a thesis about the part our relations with other human beings play in our own well-being. By this line of argument, I hope to show that the conflict between self-interest and a concern for other human beings takes on a quite different aspect from the one it usually bears. My thesis will be that our *Mitsein* yields not only a deontological principle along the lines already developed but an axiological one as well. Other human beings would thus not just impose limits on what we may permissibly do; they would be essentially connected to the sources of our own well-being.

In this section, however, it is the negative side of this whole matter (and especially the character and sources of moral evil) that has to be discussed.

1 The Greek word *stasis* means "standing" or "stationariness" and also the place where one stands; and it is perhaps best known as a word for division or faction. The etymological linkage of "division" with the verb "to stand" suggests a picture in which opposing parties have taken their "stand" and cannot move any closer to one another. At any rate, that is the sense in which I use the word *stasis*; and it is intended to convey – to use a different metaphor – a kind of freezing of human relationships at a certain level of mutuality beyond which they cannot move.

A word about self-interest may help to introduce this discussion. In one respect, it is the foundation of this whole scheme of *Mitsein*. If we did not care – each of us – about ourselves, there would be no possibility of our caring about anyone else. It would be strange, after all, if some Alter Ego were to make a claim for equivalent treatment on an Ego that was indifferent to its own well-being. But in another respect self-interest is also the chief obstacle in the way of any genuine recognition of the equivalence of one human life with another. The reason for this would appear to lie in our history and in the extremely hard time we have had just surviving in the course of it. We think of our early history as having taken place in what we call the state of nature – a condition that still largely obtains in the relations of one human society with another. There can be no doubt that *Mitsein* characterized that state just as it does life in a society with political and legal institutions that are supposed to achieve some degree of public justice in the relations of human beings with one another. It is safe to assume, however, that in circumstances in which our lives were in more or less constant danger from human and other predators, any effective disposition to acknowledge the equivalence of one human life with another must have been weak at best. Nor is it likely that this changed completely when a political and legal order did emerge. Accordingly, insofar as the authority of such institutions does not rest simply on force, it has typically been judged on the narrow basis of its bearing on the self-interest of each person subject to it.

Another way of putting this would be to say that the passage from a state of nature to that of a well-ordered society is never really complete. This shows itself above all in the fact that the norms that define such a society can be exploited by the kind of unyielding priority of self-interest that is supposed to have been left behind in the state of nature but usually is not. It would hardly be too much to say that the effect of this motive is to distort the life of an ethical community to the point where what was supposed to be a partnership in a common undertaking becomes a deadlock – a *stasis* – in which both sides are trapped and from which they are quite unable to release themselves or their opposite numbers. In these circumstances, the expectations that a life ordered by cooperative arrangements would maximize the benefits enjoyed by all stands little chance of being realized. As I will show, this fact then calls forth a variety of reactions that make the prospect of a harmonious common life even more problematic.

A brief account of the way wrongdoing finds a place in the life of a community in which responsibility and trust inform our practices is in order here. This is a Hobbesian tale, and though Hobbes's telling of it remains unrivaled, it bears retelling. (What is missing from Hobbes's account is, of course, an acknowledgment of the fact of *Mitsein* in anything like the range of implication that has been set forth here; and this gives his view a powerful simplicity that an account like mine inevitably lacks.) The fundamental fact here is that even at our best, our sense of the reality of other lives and of their equivalence with our own is unstable and liable to notable intermittences, even though, in a deeper sense, it is, as I have argued, indefeasible. In unsettled or hazardous conditions, this equivalence is experienced only in its negative, Hobbesian aspect: others present the same kind of danger to me that I do to them. Self-interest, by contrast, is, if anything, intensified by just these conditions and can be counted on to be quite regularly on the job.

This is the legacy of the state of nature, in which, as we imagine it, all of us would have to be in a constant state of vigilance against human and other predators and our willingness to rely on any favorable presumptions about what other people are going to do that may affect us will be minimal. Inevitably, it would make us unwilling to go first in any cooperative exchange, since the other party might very well not do his part once we had done ours. But when we do enter into relationships of trust in an organized society, this kind of vigilance is relaxed; and this has the advantage of enabling us to get on with other, more valuable aspects of our lives instead of perpetually standing guard. Sad to say, however, this is precisely what makes us more vulnerable than we would otherwise be. Our not standing guard may make it possible for someone else to rob us or mistreat us in some way that we might well have been able to detect and block if we had not been lulled into inattention by the trust we repose in these persons. The door is thus opened to an exploitation for selfish ends of the very relationship of trust that was to ensure peaceful cooperation. The effect of such practices on the willingness of those who have suffered under them to trust anyone again is not hard to imagine. A cycle of negative reinforcement is set in motion that is at least as potent and as resistant to change as the encouragement we receive when our recognition of the equivalence of another life to our own is reciprocated.

These observations invite further reflection on the way we respond to the reality of other lives that are revealed to us under conditions of *Mitsein*. The first point that needs to be made here is that much remains the same as it would otherwise be – that is, as it would be if we had simply remained in the relation to one another in which other animals live.[2] We are still necessitous beings that have to satisfy our needs as best we can; and the conditions under which we have to do so are still set by the fact that we are competing with one another for all sorts of scarce goods. Then, too, situations are always arising in which we are competing with one another for some good that is not

---

2 Current discussion among students of animal behavior appears to favor the idea that the only imperative to which it is subject is that of seeing to it that one's own genes survive into the next generation. Among sociobiologists like E. O. Wilson, this is thought to be the case in human communities as well. See his *On Human Nature* (Cambridge, Mass.: Harvard University Press, 1978).

shareable and we may not get what we want without taking advantage of some other human being. Under these circumstances, there is great pressure on whatever bonds of trust may exist between us and our rivals. The latter are, of course, the people who have learned to expect that a justification is owed them for what we do that relevantly affects them. At the same time, they are the people from whom we have to fear the same kind of aggression that we ourselves may come to feel we have to undertake against them. This means that we are involved at one and the same time in two quite different "games" with other people and so there is always a question as to which of these will be subordinated to the other or even absorbed by it.

All this makes it hardly surprising that the kind of human world in which we live from day to day and in which – paradoxically and somewhat discreditably – we feel most at home should have the kind of hybrid character that observers of human nature have so often commented on. It is a world in which the commitment of the human beings who inhabit it to any set of understandings based on mutual recognition is never very secure and in which, as was pointed out earlier, quite inconsistent life policies may alternate within a single life with bewildering frequency.[3] The ethical reality of such lives is neither that of an unalloyed state of nature nor that of a true moral community along the lines that have been described, but rather a confused mixture of the two.[4] We may view this condition optimistically as a transitional one brought about by a movement from the state of nature to true moral community or pessimistically as a proof of the epiphenomenal character of any such normative constraints on an underlying *conatus vivendi*. As things stand, however, we are not in a position to decide this question unambiguously one way or the other. Consequently, we are compelled to live with the peculiar uncertainty that attaches to the status of the very commitments that we would like to think of as being irrevocable amd free of all ambiguity.

It needs to be emphasized that this is not just a matter of our being unavoidably uncertain about what other people may do. If we are candid with ourselves, we will have to acknowledge that we, too, on occasion may feel compelled to adopt a purely self-regarding attitude in which "responsibility"

---

3 If there is any doubt about the instability of the ways in which we relate to one another, it seems to me that the horrifying reports that have come out of the Bosnian conflict should make the point once and for all. We hear of people who have been peaceful neighbors for many years turning into rapists and murderers overnight.

4 Alasdair MacIntyre has argued in his *After Virtue* (South Bend, Ind.: Notre Dame University Press, 1981) that in the modern period morality has suffered an eclipse of disastrous proportions, largely as a result of the disintegrative influence of liberalism and liberal economics on traditional moral communities. Without wishing to dismiss the special damage that may have been done along the lines MacIntyre describes, I cannot help wondering whether he does not idealize those older moral traditions in a way that does less than justice to the conflicts by which they were riven.

and "trust" figure at best as psychological variables in a self-interested, "real-world" calculation of likelihoods of performance. Even so, it is not as though this state of affairs were enough to make trust and responsibility completely impossible. We go on trusting one another selectively and cautiously and we often formalize the engagements into which we enter in ways that entail public penalties for nonperformance. Overall, however, a world in which mistrust is an unavoidable accompaniment of trust remains a deeply equivocal one in which the status – the reality – of the relationships that derive from trust can never be completely beyond the range of doubt. Indeed, it is not too much to say that, in the larger world of affairs and of relationships between institutions, this uncertainty is so pervasive and so potentially damaging that only legally enforceable agreements have any real meaning. Even the law itself, however, though it seems such a solid reality to us most of the time, can offer little protection when the whole frame of our relationships to other people is called into question.

One way in which people deal with these matters is to conclude that these relations of trust and responsibility belong in the private sphere of family and friends and that it is unrealistic to expect them to apply to any wider community. Because relationships based on responsibility and trust are anything but easy to establish in any circumstances and because we have so often been disillusioned by fraudulent representations suggesting that someone is prepared for a cooperative relationship who in fact is not, the only safe way to go about such matters is arguably to confine the range of the ethical constraints deriving from *Mitsein* to persons whom we have other, stronger reasons to expect to comply with them. Typically, this line of thought leads to a strong disposition to trust only those to whom one stands in a fairly close personal relationship and this often means people with whom there are ties of kinship and "blood." In some societies this can give rise to a system of what has aptly been called "amoral familism."[5] In such a system, everyone who stands outside a particular circle of kinship is deemed ineligible for any relationship that carries with it a moral claim that someone within the circle has to acknowledge.[6] It is interesting to note, however, that in spite of the greatly restricted character of the trust that can be extended under these auspices the authority of the obligations deriving from it is made to rest on an identity between the parties concerned. Because that identity consists in

5 This term was first used by Edward Banfield in his *The Moral Basis of a Backward Society* (Glencoe, Ill.: Free Press, 1958), in which he describes the moral economy of Sicilian society.
6 It has also been shown that such attitudes have a profound effect, not only, as one would expect, on the political life of the societies in which they are widely shared but upon economic life as well, most notably the likelihood that large economic institutions can be founded that depend upon cooperation and trust among persons with no ties of kinship or even friendship. See Francis Fukuyama, *Trust: The Social Virtues and the Creation of Prosperity* (New York: Free Press, 1995).

being members of the same family or clan, it is far narrower than, and very differently conceived from, the identity with one another that was described in Chapter 1. The key difference, of course, remains: one attitude is universal, at least in principle, and the other is a modified form of egoistic particularism.

Kinship is not, of course, the only basis on which this kind of restricted moral economy can be made to rest. Large (and small) institutions of all kinds can adopt similar policies while trying to make it appear that they are far more open to the claims of their fellow human beings than they really are. All this adds up to a form of social life that is characterized by a disposition to stand on positions of strength already achieved and an extreme reluctance to take chances on people outside one's own mafias. This attitude very readily reinforces and reproduces itself. This, in turn, makes it very difficult for anyone to have an experience of a form of life in which responsibility and trust are solidly established as the pervasive modalities of human relationships. To this it must be added that the experience a great many people do have is one of the actual neglect of the obligations owed to them by those who bear the corresponding responsibilities. What is perhaps most remarkable about human beings is the fact that in spite of such experiences so many of them are still able to believe in the reality of a moral bond between human beings.

These considerations suggest a more general point about the moral economy of such a world as the one I have been describing. It is not just that, as La Rochefoucauld said, hypocrisy is the homage vice pays to virtue. "Vice" or wrongdoing is parasitic in an even stronger sense upon virtue if the latter is understood to include a willingness to rely on the undertakings of others. In other words, the very possibility of wrongdoing is dependent on there being in place something like a common norm of expectation in relation to which certain actions have to count as violations. It is true that one human being can simply overpower and kill another even if there is no special understanding between them. This is the kind of thing that animals constantly do to one another; and though we are often appalled by it, we would typically hesitate to call it wrong. An explanation of the distinction we thereby make would, I think, make the matter turn on the presumptive absence in the animal case of the kind of mutual recognition that is at the heart of *Mitsein*. Among human beings, by contrast, wrongdoing normally presupposes a context that is set by certain inhibitions against predatory conduct; and it takes advantage of the trust we repose in one another on the strength of these inhibitions. It would, accordingly, be quite in order to speak with Saint Augustine, though in a nontheological sense, of a priority of good over evil on the grounds that good as the coming into being of a framework of mutual recognition is a necessary condition for the possibility of a violation of the ethical relationships predicated upon it.

It might be questioned whether, in the kind of "hybrid" state I have been describing, it is really possible to speak of responsibility and trust at all. Can we really be said to trust someone whom we also feel we may have to take precautions against? Perhaps the only answer that can be given to this question is, "Well, yes and no." Although this answer is unlikely to satisfy anyone who asks the original question, the equivocal condition it brings to expression is a reality – the reality, it might be suggested – of our moral lives. It is one in which the authority we claim for ethical requirements of various kinds is in one sense unconditional and independent of our wills, but at the same time is not something we can rely upon without incurring unacceptable risks unless others do so as well. Most people would consider it to be unreasonable to take the risks that may be involved in honoring an obligation when there is real reason to think that our action will not be reciprocated. On this view, an element of the conditional must be acknowledged in the obligation to others that is implicit in *Mitsein*. This reflects the fact that an obligation may apply to others as well as to oneself and compliance with it has to be predicated on their willingness to respond appropriately. Another way of putting this would be to say that the authority of that obligation is always presumptive and that the presumption in question is rebuttable when our partners are not prepared to comply with the requirements of the situation.

There is a further complexity here. When doubts arise about the willingness of someone else to play his part in the moral relationship that I recognize and am prepared to honor, and I – that is, each of us – must judge the matter for myself, there is always the possibility that, at the bidding of a narrowly (and perhaps foolishly) conceived self-interest, this will be done in a disingenuous way. As a result, a situation may arise in which the other party, who surmises what I am doing, may very well draw the same negative conclusions about me that I am drawing about him and with as much or more justification. In fact, everyone in this situation may think of himself as being willing in principle to enter a fair cooperative arrangement with the others and as being prevented from doing so by the absence of a comparable willingness on the other side. But all these judgments have a strong tendency to be self-serving; and bad faith in the estimating of the willingness of others to cooperate with us can bring about the same result as an unrepentant selfishness would. In these circumstances, it is a question whether there is anything in *Mitsein* that can break this deadlock. If there is not, the authority of the distinctively ethical view of such situations will inevitably suffer and the whole ethical enterprise will have to look a good deal more precarious to us than we are ordinarily willing to admit. But unless we are prepared to claim that the reality of wrongdoing presupposes no context of mutual recognition at all, this precariously situated ordering of our lives in terms of relationships of responsibility and trust provides the only basis for ethical judgment we have.

This situation may be said to set another ethical problem for us at a different level from the one at which our primary recognition of other human beings occurs and, with it, our sense of the ethical implications of the relation in which we stand to them. The level is different because, in addition to the sheer fact of *Mitsein*, it presupposes an understanding of the unstable condition of such effective ethical reciprocity as may be said to exist. A decision has to be taken here that, by its very nature, has to be made without any completely reliable sense of being supported in it by other similarly situated human beings who face the same choice. In other words, the sheer fact of the plurality of distinct persons who have to make this choice between the state of nature and a compliance with the ethical import of *Mitsein* adds a dimension of uncertainty to the choice each of us has to make in circumstances in which an unsupported adherence to the latter may carry risks for one's own interests and, indeed, for oneself.

When our moral situation is envisaged in these stark terms, which, by the way, we normally do our best to avoid, what stands out most clearly is that there can be no reliable guarantee that compliance with "the moral point of view" will be conducive to personal well-being as we ordinarily understand it. But in that case, the rationale by which the claims of morality are made to rest on enlightened self-interest begins to look a little shaky; and when that happens, people are very likely to reassess their commitment to what Hume called the "moral institution." It may even begin to look as though the claims it makes are indices of the kind of weakness with which Nietzsche and Plato's Thrasymachus identified the moral interest. In any case, the apparent powerlessness of an ordering of life on the basis of responsibility and trust must be deeply upsetting to those who have counted on it as a means to their own happiness.

This disappointment can easily turn into contempt. When this happens, it will be difficult to avoid the conclusion that the ethical enterprise is at best a pious fraud – a disingenuous attempt to disguise the actual nature of the relationships that prevail among human beings. To those who take this view, this is a dog-eat-dog world in which no one really takes ethical considerations seriously or as anything but window-dressing for people's real motives and purposes. This is the vision of social life that Thrasymachus and Callicles espouse: a form of life in which moral considerations do not represent anyone's primary understanding of the good and function mainly, if not exclusively, as a means by which the weak keep the strong from doing exactly as they please. When violators are caught *in flagrante delicto* and exposed to public view, they suffer the consequences of acting publicly in the way that everyone, privately, would prefer to act if he were strong enough. On this view, morality is a kind of myth that has to be maintained as a cover for everyone's real purposes and that can, incidentally, be turned to advantage as a way of discrediting one's rivals. It is not difficult to identify attitudes in our own time that are very much in this spirit and express admiration for the strong and for the way they ride roughshod over the inhibitions under which lesser beings labor.[7]

There is still another step that this devaluation of the ethical attitude can take. Even though, on such a view, there neither is nor can be any such thing as true moral obligation, it is assumed that when one's own purposes are detrimental to those of others, this fact must be concealed and, if necessary, denied. This is because the trust of those simple enough to be deceived and who stand to lose as a result of something one has in mind to do, must be maintained and, where necessary, encouraged as a necessary condition for the success of what one is proposing to do. From this, it is just a step to the final perversion of *Mitsein* – the step beyond wrongdoing to what can only be called "evil." What I have been calling wrongdoing involves taking advantage of relationships of trust that already exist. It is something else to encourage and even create such relationships so that they can then be exploited for purposes that are alien to them. Such practices evince an explicit understanding of the form of life that is based on responsibility and trust and they make that understanding a means to the achievement of purposes that are quite amoral in character. This amounts to a discrediting of what is arguably the one fragile chance we have to emerge unambiguously from the state of nature in our relations with one another; and it is a perversion that has already done much to destroy that chance.

Philosophers have often posed the question of whether it is possible to do evil intentionally. What has just been said supplies the basis for an affirmative answer to that question; but it has to be understood in the right way. "Evil," as I am using the term, denotes what someone does intentionally to pervert a system of human cooperation based on mutual recognition by making it an instrument of private and intrinsically unshareable purposes. The use of this term thus presupposes that there is such a system, however imperfect, in being. It is this assumption that is ostensibly not shared by the person who creates trust only to exploit it. For whatever reason, he is convinced that people generally stand in the peculiarly distanced and potentially exploitative relation to ethical constraints that has been described here. People never really accept those constraints and the pretense that they do is simply designed to fool the gullible. But in that case it follows that, in tricking others, one is only making use of a myth of their own making in order to beat them at their own game. A solemn term like "evil" may be used to describe this tactic; but it too reflects the delusory belief that there is really something in being that is perverted by the conduct it is used to describe.

---

7 In the 1970s many books were published that told people that they should not be held back by considerations of morality in furthering their careers. Typical of this literature was the work of one Robert J. Ringer, whose titles include *Winning Through Intimidation, Looking Out For Number One,* and so on.

In other words, what someone who accepts that belief calls doing evil intentionally would really reduce to doing "evil" intentionally – that is, to doing what someone else calls evil out of false assumptions about human nature. The quotation marks show that the agent is using someone else's description for what he has done and also that he does not accept the presuppositions required in order to give that description any real basis in fact.

All this may be so and yet it is hard not to conclude that there is a very considerable element of bad faith in the case I have just imagined such people making for themselves. It rests altogether on claims about the basically amoral character of the actions and the motives of other human beings. It is easy to imagine someone who has suffered at the hands of other human beings, perhaps because he was made vulnerable by the trust he placed in them, reacting against the whole system of mutuality by reason of its partial and imperfect character. The trouble is that however understandable a disillusionment of this kind may be, it can lead straight into an attitude that is quite untenable. It is as though such a person has supposed himself to be the beneficiary of a system of moral cooperation that is in full operation and into which he had simply been dropped as if from outer space. Consequently, he lacks any sense of a commitment to maintain its equilibrium against the multiple hazards to which it is in fact exposed. When he is disappointed as a result of someone else's exploitation of his trust, he claims the same "right" as this exploiter to treat any and all inhibitions on conduct in a purely instrumental way. This means that he would be free to disregard their manifest import whenever that would serve his own interest. Such a reaction naturally makes whatever degree of effective mutuality has been achieved even more imperfect and thus, in a paradoxical way, appears to justify itself. But by taking this course, he also cuts the ground out from under his own case. He cannot justify his own actions by pointing to those of others when he responds to the latter with actions that are at least as bad as theirs are.

The point I am making here is that the sort of individual I am postulating is trying to have things both ways. He is playing the part of the hyper-realist who is disabused of all illusions about other people's motives and dismisses all their pretenses of respect for ethical constraints. But at the same time he offers a justification for what he is doing that in effect addresses these persons as though they could grasp the validity – the *bien-fondé* – of the case he is making. Since any meaningful capacity to judge such matters across the lines that separate one life from another cannot be governed solely by the reflexes of self-interest, our individual is evidently relying on the very *Mitsein* that he is also repudiating; and it is in this sense that he is trying to have things both ways. Nor is this just a bit of carelessness about the logic of his own position. If that were all that is wrong, it could simply be cleared up by his not making any statement at all, implicit or explicit, about what he is doing. But this would be to act as though there were no one there – no Alter – to whom such a statement could be addressed; and this would be to try to cancel out the fact of *Mitsein* itself – something that no one can do. In a very deep way, then, the position of such a person is incoherent and is in fact parasitic on the very *Mitsein* it is trying to deny.

To this it may be added, at a lower level of abstraction, that it would be very surprising if such persons were truly consistent and, in accordance with their own declared principles, never tried to avail themselves – straightforwardly – of the assistance offered by the very system of reciprocity, imperfect as it is, that they claim to have seen through. In this way, once again, the position of those who exploit and pervert whatever cooperative practices are in existence reveals a deep inconsistency that must weaken its claim to be the final, illusion-free truth about these matters. The rationale that is offered for this line of conduct is, after all, impervious to refutation only because it attempts to be resolutely solipsistic. It succeeds, however, only in sinking to a kind of ground-zero of *Mitsein* at which other people are, unavoidably, acknowledged but treated as having no reality as human beings.[8] Incoherent though it may be, this stance can sometimes be associated with a terrible energy that expresses itself in a fierce hatred of everything and everyone that suggests there are moral limits that we do not set for ourselves. As the novels of Dostoyevsky and indeed the political history of our own century show us, this attitude can manifest itself in the political domain with predictably devastating consequences when the idea that "everything is permitted" becomes the rationale for crime and terrorism.

What I have been trying to describe in this section is a downward slide that leads to the perversion of the relationships of responsibility and trust on which a moral community is founded. As I noted at the outset, this process brings about a situation in which people may fairly be described as having trapped one another and themselves. This is because all the remedies one might think of as being capable of bringing things "into the true" must now be scrutinized from a strategic point of view. This means that they will be viewed with the suspicion that is appropriate when moves are made in a zero-sum game; and as a result any recognition of the fact that one side is as trapped as the other will be very unlikely and certainly not a perception of their situation that could be shared by both parties. As far as I can tell, this situation in which the moral life itself becomes a pawn in a contest that really has no rules has not received the attention it deserves from contemporary moralists.[9] This is regrettable since the life policies that base themselves

8 For an interpretation of autism as a pathological inability to understand other persons as having "mental" states, see S. Baron-Cohen, *Mindblindness* (Cambridge, Mass.: MIT Press, 1995).

9 It is somewhat startling to discover, for example, that in one of the few books by a philosopher on this topic, John Kekes's *Facing Evil* (Princeton, N.J.: Princeton University Press, 1990), no notice is taken of the kind of evil I discuss in this book. It might be suggested that

on such a view of our moral situation are not, if I am right, as impervious to refutation as they are often supposed to be, nor does this refutation require an appeal to some basis for ethical authority that lies completely outside the kind of dialectic I have been describing.

II

The account just given of our moral situation makes it appropriate to ask what resources, if any, may be available to human nature for dealing with it.[10] If there are such resources, they must be adequate to show how one could be motivated to "go first," that is, to honor the moral requirements of *Mitsein,* even under conditions in which there is no assurance of reciprocation by others and there may be real risks to one's own interests in going ahead alone. What we are talking about here is a source of motivation in human nature that is strong enough to persist in the face of the abuse and even the radical perversion of ethical relationships among human beings that have just been described. In these circumstances the motive in question evidently cannot be self-interest in any familiar sense, although that presumably is what motivates compliance with those requirements under the very different conditions of a "well-ordered society." Finding such a motive is

a book like Josiah Royce's *The Philosophy of Loyalty* could help to correct the perspective we bring to bear on the facts of the moral life; and the same might be said of his *The Problem of Christianity.* One suspects that resistance to taking evil seriously may have its roots in the kind of liberalism that was informed by the doctrine of American exceptionalism and the sense that as a new nation we had "put off the old man" and with him the sinful ways of the old world. On such a view, the idea itself of obligation or "being bound" is linked with a suspicious and punitive view of human nature; and, by parity of reasoning, a true human community in which a natural harmony of benign feelings and purposes prevails is not likely to come into being unless such ideas are given up. R. W. B. Lewis has given an account of these beliefs in *The American Adam: Innocence, Tragedy and Tradition in the Nineteenth Century* (Chicago: University of Chicago Press, 1955).

I may also note that, even farther back, Dante's classification of the forms of moral wrong in his *Inferno* and the central place that he assigns to malice (*malitia*) and to its worst form, treachery, still have something important to say to us. See Joan Ferrante's excellent book, *The Political Vision of the Divine Comedy* (Princeton, N.J.: Princeton University Press, 1984).

10 Although Hobbes was our guide to this downward slide, his view of the only effective remedy in such a case is not likely to be of comparable value for this inquiry. He argued that the only rational course for people in a world like ours is to make over all their powers of decision to a single sovereign authority whose word, backed by a monopoly of collective force, would be binding on all. In this way they could at least ensure peace amongst themselves and avoid the horrors of civil war. This remedy assumes that civil peace is achievable only by moving all the issues between us to another level at which there is only a single arbiter and that the most important thing is not so much how these issues are resolved but that they be resolved at all (and in a way that is enforceable). It is doubtful, however, whether it would be easier to achieve agreement on such a decision-making system than it would on substantive issues; and so the difficulty remains.

plainly not going to be an easy task. Even so, I propose to argue that there are resources in human nature that make such conduct possible, although just how effective the actions they motivate will be is hard to judge.

It seems clear that if *Mitsein* is hollowed out and finally corrupted by the tactics of self-interest described in the preceding section, a remedy for this state of affairs must depend on an ability on our part to understand this same *Mitsein* of ours in a new dimension. It has already been characterized as a matrix of joint inquiry and thus of truth; and it has also been shown to be the ground of ethics in the sense that it constitutes a relation of equivalence from which a set of limits on what we may do in our relation to one another also derives. What is now required is that *Mitsein* be shown to be deeply implicated in the conditions of our own and everyone's well-being or happiness. What this amounts to is a claim that the happiness of each one of us stands in a relation of interdependence to that of others, so that the well-being of Alter cannot in principle be indifferent to that of Ego, even if there is no sign of a reciprocating interest on Alter's part. Unless this can be persuasively shown, it would not make sense for anyone to "go first" in the kind of situation described in the last section and to take the risks that involves. It would make no sense because there would be no general presumption that a linkage exists between Ego's well-being and Alter's, although on occasion a particular consideration of self-interest might dictate a favorable attitude.

It is just such a presumption that I want to justify at this point. It would mean that our natures comprise a set of dispositions, more or less widely shared, that assign an essential place in our understanding of the good to mutuality in our relations to our fellow human beings and that these dispositions enjoy at least a degree of independence from the other kinds of things that are usually thought to constitute our well-being. That this is not simply a chimerical hope is shown by the fact that mutuality already has some place in the good as it is understood by almost everyone. Usually, however, the circle of those who figure in our lives in such a way as to give mutuality this status is quite restricted; and even then it may be in the service of an unacknowledged self-interest. It is only when that circle opens on wider and wider areas of association with others that there is much chance of breaking out of the *stasis* I described in the last section. But almost everything we know about ourselves suggests that even when that happens, it cannot be realistically expected that the full intensity of our sense of identity with others can be preserved as it moves outward from those who are very close to us to those whom we mostly do not know at all. There are certainly people who have achieved a degree of compassionate identification with such persons that greatly exceeds our normal level. But what reason do most of us have for thinking that this sort of thing does not simply lie beyond our own powers? And even if that is not the case, would not the risks this kind of nonreciprocated beneficence entails make it foolhardy and even irrational as a life policy? Before opening up this topic by a review of some relevant areas of moral philosophy, I want to touch briefly on a very different approach to the matters I am discussing. I have in mind the injunction in the New Testament to love our neighbor as we do ourselves. In this passage the word for "love" – in the Authorized Version it is translated as "charity" from the Latin *caritas* – is the Greek word *agape,* not *eros.*[11] I mention this because there is a question about what word would best convey the character of the mode of feeling toward other people that is at issue here. I have proposed "caring-about" as a rendering of Heidegger's *Fürsorge;* it has definite advantages over "love," with its connotations of romantic and sexual passion. Even so, it is a bit on the anemic side; and the Greek *agape* has much richer nuances of meaning, some of which seem to me to be applicable to this situation. Unlike eros, which suggests a passionate and possessive attachment, *agape* is a love divorced from desire and undeterred by the great, often unattractive commonalities of our human nature.[12] It acknowledges our shared condition of life and our profound similarities across all the lines that normally divide us; and it is able to respond to this often quite grim perception of our lives with a measure of hope. It is the kind of perception that has what I can only call our "creatureliness" as its object. This word, of course, suggests the drawback of *agape* as a word for this feeling – the fact, namely, that it is closely tied to the notion of a creator and his presumptive feelings toward his "creatures." Here I can only appeal to the queer sort of Feuerbachian logic by which we reappropriate a notion of which we must, after all, already have had some understanding before attributing it to the creator we postulate. In

---

11 "Charity" comes from *caritas* via the Old French *cherté.* This word for the dearness to us of someone or something also served to denote the affection or love we have for that someone or something.

By invoking the notion of love in this context, I clearly cannot claim to be elaborating any theme that Heidegger develops, but at the same time there is nothing in his thought that rules out the introduction of this concept. The only discussion of the place of love in Heidegger's thought that I am familiar with is in the unpublished doctoral dissertation of Holger Helting at the University of Vienna, "Studien und Quellenforschung zum undurchdachten Verhaltnis zwischen Sokrates, Platon, und Heidegger," ch. 1D, "Liebe zum Mitmenschen als Vollendung des 'Daseins' bzw. des Selbst bei Heidegger und Kierkegaard." Helting takes a very positive view of the role of love in Heidegger's account of the emergence of an authentic self and he backs up his view with some very significant quotations from Heidegger's writings.

12 Anders Nygren, *Eros and Agape,* translated by Philip Watson (Philadelphia: Westminster Press, 1953), has been helpful to me in my attempt to understand the concept of *agape,* although Nygren argues that only God is capable of this kind of love. One important difference between a divine and a human *agape* would surely have to do with forgiveness. An acceptance of human frailty cannot require that we forgive those who not only do grave harm to others but repudiate the whole spirit of mutuality on which the very idea of morality rests.

any case, I want to be able to equate the "caring-for" I have in mind with the kind of perception and feeling for one another that the word *agape* expresses. I do so because it seems to me to be much more appropriate to a moral condition as equivocal as our own than are the bursts of life-affirming enthusiasm that have been characteristic of some of the more familiar traditions of melioristic thought.

First among the relevant topics of moral philosophy to which I want to turn now is the concept itself of the good as the foundation of our notions of well-being and happiness. The most natural way of thinking of the good is as the object of desire. There are, of course, questions that need to be asked about whether something we desire can really satisfy our desire and whether our desire itself may not be, in some degree, the product of illusion. This kind of critical scrutiny of a first adumbration of the good can lead to substantial modifications of it; but it is generally assumed that, however extensive these may be, their end result will be something that I can still desire and that that desire will motivate my pursuit of that good. In keeping with these assumptions, the concept of the good has been widely understood, especially in the modern period, as defining forms of satisfaction that may be subject to judgment in light of some other standard, but need not be (and typically are not) themselves inherently ethical in character.

That "other standard" has traditionally been the principle of right; and it is with that principle that the concept of the good has usually been paired by moralists to form the great dichotomy that organizes their discipline. Indeed, it is to this principle that most moralists would probably think we should turn in attempting to deal with the kind of impasse described in the preceding section; and I bring it into this discussion at this point mainly to show why that would not be a good idea. Unlike the good, the notion of what is right carries no immediately attractive associations with it. What it invokes in the first instance is a situation in which something contravenes our own desire: the will of God, a parent's authority, the law of the land, or the categorical imperative. Most commonly, when a desire that intends a good of some kind is ruled out by one of these authorities, it is on the grounds that that desire, if acted on, would harm someone else. Other people are thus envisaged as limits on what we may do and those limits are what the concept of the right is supposed to define. In keeping with these assumptions, the concept of the good has been widely understood, especially in the modern period, as defining forms of satisfaction that may be subject to judgment in light of the principle of right, but need not be (and typically are not) themselves inherently ethical in character. It is widely held, therefore, that the concept of the right must constitute the quintessentially ethical element in our lives. Nevertheless, the motivation on which it must draw in order to be effective has remained obscure.

It may indeed be difficult to be enthusiastic about the kind of rectitude that is associated with the principle of right, but the history of moral philosophy shows that it is not impossible. A long line of moralists, from the Stoics to Immanuel Kant, have reserved their highest encomia for just the kind of self-denial that the principle of right requires of us. Even so, there is something rather paradoxical about this praise. It appears to presuppose the familiar contrast between a life of enjoyment that is largely independent of moral inhibitions and a strenuously conceived moral rectitude; our rational natures are held to be allied with the latter and indeed to require of us that we live in conformity to the moral law. But this contrast is then turned around in such a way that the right and doing one's duty will come to seem even more attractive to us than the kind of happiness that these moralists tend to identify with the gross pleasures of the senses. The case is made that our respect for the moral law generates a respect for ourselves as moral beings; and this sense of our own dignity as moral beings is supposed to compensate us for the sacrifice we have made of other modes of pleasurable feeling that do not have their source, as this one is held to, in our higher faculties.[13] In this way, the good implicit in this kind of feeling about ourselves tacitly supplies the motive for a compliance with the requirements of the principle of right. It does so, however, in a way that involves an appeal to something good that comes our way when we conform to the principle of right, and thereby plainly violates the identification of the latter with the purely formal or logical elements in our practical rationality.

The conclusion I would draw from all this is that the principle of right is a principle of criticism and not of motivation – not, at any rate, until it has been shown to be connected with something that has the character of a good. This would suggest that the principle of right needs to be openly brought under the same roof, so to speak, with the idea of the good. But if, as I have been arguing, the central axis of the moral life is our developing understanding of the implications of the fact that there are other human beings in the world with us, then some other possibilities can be entertained. Most notably, there is the possibility that our *Mitsein* could generate not just rules that give effect to the underlying equivalence of one human life with another but another kind of mutuality as well that makes another's happiness a condition, in some significant degree, of one's own. Generically, that kind of mutuality is present wherever human beings are able to care about

13 Even though Kant's case against our affective natures as a basis for moral distinctions is a powerful one, so is the counterargument offered by Friedrich Schiller. After all, it can hardly be denied that someone whose feelings incline him to compliance with moral requirements is a far more attractive human being than the one who complies with gritted teeth. Even now when Kant's rigorism has little appeal, the way in which the contrast between the good and the right is understood by philosophers bears the mark of his influence. See E. M. Wilkinson and L. A. Willoughby, eds., *Friedrich Schiller: On the Aesthetic Education of Man* (Oxford: Clarendon Press, 1967).

or love one another, although the number of such persons is typically, in the case of each of us, quite small. By contrast, our relation to almost everyone else has been long dominated by fear. The real question is thus whether or not it is possible to widen the scope of such mutuality in such a way that our *Mitsein* is not just an unstable equilibrium but a relation in which our well-being is positively enhanced by the well-being of a much larger number of people than we currently care about.

I now want to see if this train of thought cannot be connected to a consideration of the good understood as a condition of well-being or happiness. The first point that needs to be made is that we tend to think about happiness in quite different ways. One of these conceives happiness in terms of the enjoyable experiences that come our way, sometimes through our own efforts but also as a result of the natural lottery that assigns health, beauty, and special talents to us and makes us the children of just these parents and not others. This might be called happiness as it is understood from the point of view of the "consumer" of these experiences. But when we think of happiness in a less passive way and more from the standpoint of the person who has to order his life in one way or another, it makes more sense to understand happiness as the fulfillment of a lifelong purpose that expresses the character of the individual in question. These two ways of thinking about happiness are not mutually exclusive. No life can be entirely subordinate to a plan, and all of us seek enjoyments that may be extrinsic to such plans as we have. And even those who best fit the model of happiness as consumption project a future for themselves that reflects their preferences in such matters.

Nevertheless, the difference between the two remains important if only because the first one lends itself so much more readily to a conception of one person's well-being as independent of and separate from that of another. In the one case, it is clear that the well-being of one person can coexist with the deprivation and misery of another without any perceptible strain, since these are discrete experiences and are not predicated on one another. This is because the fundamental relation between human beings is understood as a side-by-side relation in which consumption and enjoyment and their opposites are in each case episodes in the life of these people. It may be the case that one such individual is particularly sensitive to the suffering or the happiness of others; but this would count as a psychological fact about that individual and would be fitted accordingly into the same general scheme. In the other picture, there is a much better chance that happiness as fulfillment will at least bring the conditions of one person's happiness into a definable relation to those of other people and thus establish an interdependence between them. The effect would thus be to tie one human being to others in a way that has a bearing on the question posed at the beginning of this section.

It seems clear that the fulfillment concept of happiness has substantial advantages over the consumption concept. Certainly it is the common testimony of mankind that a life can be filled with enjoyable experiences and still be hollow and, what is worse, empty. Happiness surely means some kind of fulfillment in an individual life that goes beyond having eaten so many splendid meals or any other aggregate of enjoyments one can put together over a span of years. But what is more important for present purposes is the fact that the moment we think of happiness in terms of fulfillment this picture changes. It changes because in the matter of such fulfillments our relation to other human beings and to their well-being plays a very prominent role. Not only are they very likely to impinge upon other lives in a way that affects their quality for good or ill; our sense of the value of what we are trying to accomplish is finally contingent upon the response we get from other people and especially from those who are supposed to benefit from what we do. It is certainly true that there have been many life plans that appear to envisage nothing more than the self-aggrandizement of their author and yet there is almost always an appeal implicit in them to some wider audience on the grounds of a larger philanthropic intention that supposedly animates the enterprise. The point here is that we cannot certify our own worth or that of our achievements even to ourselves simply on our own say-so; and so the notion of a solipsistic fulfillment without a basis in any kind of mutuality must be an incoherent fantasy.

A compelling illustration of what I have in mind here is the way many people devote their lives to the well-being of their families. This concern for our children is perhaps the most readily available example of unselfishness as well as of the responsibility and trust discussed earlier. There is, of course, always the question of how that life goal relates to those of others who may have the same hopes for their children. It may be that to conceive a life plan and the efforts it entails in behalf of others entirely in terms of the well-being of those to whom one is close in this special way is simply too narrow. But the relevant point here is that, whatever its possible shortcomings, such a conception of the fulfillment of a life ties the happiness of its author to that of other human beings. In that sense it breaks out of any compartmentalization of well-being in a way that is analogous to that in which truth can be shared by all the participants in *Mitsein*. More concretely, a life can be fulfilled by efforts in behalf of others only if the good one does them is such that it can be acknowledged by them as a good, if not immediately, then eventually.

The claim that our happiness is dependent in a very significant degree on the responses we get from other people to the kind of thing we are trying to achieve can be made good by an appeal to evidence drawn from studies of the lives of children and their maturation. A child's sense of itself is massively dependent upon the attitudes toward it of those who care for it. More concretely, its ability to develop the positive sense of itself that is a necessary condition for an ability to project a vision of a fulfilling life depends on its feeling loved and valued by those to whom it is closest. This is not to say that when a child is not the fortunate recipient of such love, it will be permanently disabled and incapable of achieving anything worthwhile in its life. That certainly can happen; but human nature is also very resourceful in devising expedients for dealing with such situations. But even when we are successful in finding a way of living with the absence from our lives of the love and respect we need, that absence leaves its often indelible mark on those lives. When that happens, our ability to achieve (or to enjoy) the happiness we desire may be gravely affected.

But what about adulthood? Surely it is implicit in the kind of autonomy we associate with being "grown up" that we are able to discount and effectively disregard other people's attitudes toward us. And even when other people and their attitudes toward us are important to us, we must be able to find ways of dealing with defections that occur among the very people who have been close to us. All this is true; but this in many ways admirable independence is typically predicated on the hope for an eventual peripeteia in which the truth about us will become manifest and attitudes will accordingly change. In the absence of such a recognition there would always be a question, in our minds as well as in those of others, as to whether what we have accomplished was really worth doing. Once again, for all our self-sufficiency, we cannot certify our own worth, even to ourselves; and nothing can cancel out a massive, residual dependence on at least two things we greatly need. One of these is recognition of what we (are trying to) achieve in our work and in our lives, especially by those who are in a position to appreciate and understand what we are about. Unless there is such recognition, the satisfaction we get from it will inevitably be diminished. The other is the support of those who love us, especially when we fail or fall short in whatever effort it is that we are making.

There are, of course, people who insist that they can do without either of these forms of support; and even this kind of defiant self-sufficiency can serve us well on occasion. The trouble with it is that it is always in danger of hardening into a defensive carapace that imprisons us and thereby reduces our ability to enjoy recognition when it comes, if it does. It would be a rare bird indeed to whom no response from another human being to anything in his life or his work meant anything. And to this I would add that to most of us it means a great deal – so much, in fact, that it supplies the main motive for much of what we do. This is true both of the things we do that command general respect and the acquisitive and self-aggrandizing life programs that are regrettably all too common. All those expensive clothes and houses and "trophy wives" just would not mean very much if they did not call forth the envious admiration of those who share the same idea of the good.

This line of thought is not likely to meet with universal assent; there is even a considerable body of opinion that would regard it as almost the reverse of the truth. From one side, it will be objected that this version of the role of other people in our lives is a recipe for the most abject conformism – a kind of compulsory editing of our opinions and attitudes that is designed to elicit approval and agreement from others. But this objection fires from the hip. It is simply being assumed that the only motive for taking other people's views seriously is a weak-willed inability to stand up vigorously for one's own; and that is simply not the case. From another quarter, it will be said that other people are responsible for our keenest disappointments and so it must be extremely misguided to base any part of our happiness on them. This view – the "people are no damn good" thesis, as it might be called – sounds very much like a negative version of my thesis. Certainly, the fact, if it is a fact, that it is people, more than anything else, that make us unhappy tends to confirm rather than to refute my claim. Finally, it will be pointed out that many of us find our happiness by fleeing other people to the extent we can into pursuits that are as independent of them as possible. A preference for the natural world and its creatures over the social one is one form this attitude often takes just now, and a life devoted to art or science or just plain work may be another. But in all such cases it would seem that the point being made is not that the impact on our lives and our happiness of other human beings is trivial but it is so pervasively negative that we have to find alternatives to it.

On the other side of this issue, I would offer the following considerations. When our relation to other people is informed by the attitude to one another that is suggested by the idea of *agape,* the whole set of contrasts between yours and mine takes on a quite different aspect. When we truly care about another person, the rhetoric of self-denial and of our own resultant moral dignity becomes largely irrelevant. In saying this, I am not trying to invoke a special sort of moral highmindedness that would presumably turn out to be reserved to an elite of some kind. My intention, instead, is to bring into the discussion of ethical matters the contention that in the context of *Mitsein* the goods we value and seek for ourselves increasingly become what I can only call "person-related goods." This happens when we come to understand the degree to which the goods we ordinarily seek are mediated by other human beings who in one way or another help us to acquire or achieve what we want or need.[14] As the fact of this kind of mediation, which can be negative as well as positive since people can block as well as facilitate our

14 It is true that we can and often do pay for the services others render us and may, therefore, feel justified in substituting the "cash nexus" for any feelings of gratitude that would be appropriate. It is very doubtful, however, that we can clear our accounts with everyone in this way; and the attempt to do so can blight what might otherwise be very valuable experiences for us.

own efforts, comes to impress itself more deeply upon us, there is also a displacement of the deepest sources of our own personal happiness in the direction of these same relations to the human beings who have made possible the goods that we may have thought of previously only in terms of our consumption of them. In part, this recognition comes when we are able to grasp the more general fact that, with certain important exceptions, the most important things, good and bad, that happen to us in our lives are the effect of what other people do and do not do. More relevantly, what I am getting at is the fact that human beings reach their full powers only with the assistance of others and even then stand in need of the support and recognition that others can give them.

Against this background, the symmetry between these conditions of human happiness and an approach to ethics through the concept of *Mitsein* seems plain. In the preceding chapter, I argued that an obligation to act (or not act) in a certain way can arise only out of a relation to another being like ourselves; and in that sense *Mitsein* acts to restrict our options as the principle of right has been supposed to do. Along this same line of thought, I have also shown that a good that is constituted in our relations to other human beings cannot be one that is independent of ethical considerations. The reason is that it would itself be embedded in the context of *Mitsein* and thus associated with the conditions of mutuality among persons that have already been shown to be ethical in character. Because it is not premoral, as something would be that one could consume and enjoy independently of anyone else, it would not have to be checked and corrected by some authority that is external to it – the office we assign to the principle of right.

But if our *Mitsein* sets these limits, it has also been shown to be the source of the experiences that constitute the foundation of our own well-being, as it is of that of other human beings as well. Important and often essential as the other goods we seek are to us, it is only in a reciprocal relation to someone who can recognize us and confirm us in our sense of what we aspire to be that a form of happiness is realized that cannot be reduced to the private consumption of the good things this world has to offer. Instead, the enjoyment of these goods itself involves an acknowledgment of the part others have played in making them possible and thereby enhancing our lives. In some sense, then, these goods elude the kind of distinction that is normally implicit in the contrast between the good and the right – a distinction between an enjoyment that is pre-ethical and a rule that defines the rights of others that we are to respect. Instead, because the good in question here is one that is set in the context of *Mitsein,* it is (or can be) understood on all sides to be a point of intersection of the lives (and the perspectives on those lives) of two or more persons who cannot repudiate their identity with one another as this was defined in earlier chapters.

It is a pity that this whole aspect of our lives receives so little attention from the founders of existential philosophy. I suspect the reason for this is a tendency on their part to think in terms of a stern self-reliance and to conceive this kind of dependency on others as weakness. There may also be a tacit assumption at work here that a developmental conception of human life in which all the existential virtues would rest upon a certain relation to others and not simply on individual decisions cannot be reconciled with the fixed character that ontology assigns to the features of human nature it defines. As a result, although existential philosophers have had a great deal to say about death as the end of life, they have said almost nothing about birth or about infancy or childhood. It is true that Heidegger was deeply concerned with the way our lives are shaped by what is handed down to us from preceding generations. Even so, he tends to give an account of tradition that largely abstracts from the actual people who are its bearers and the role they play in the life of the child who gets its sense of itself from them. The need of the child for such persons in its life and the unavoidable dependency on them in which our lives begin is a form of finitude that, unlike our mortality, never seems to have held the interest of these philosophers.

This may be the reason why some of them, though not Heidegger, describe human beings as though they were the products of some implausible self-invention. It is, however, a non sequitur to assume that because human being – *Dasein* – is ontologically distinctive, it cannot be conceived as developing in such a way that it only achieves its mature form by stages. These stages themselves would be peculiar to the kind of entity that a human being is; and it is therefore appropriate to say that a child is a *Dasein* even though some of its powers as such cannot yet come into play. To this it might be added that it seems extremely likely that the whole phenomenon of *Das Man* could be made much more readily intelligible if set in the context of a developmental conception of human nature along the lines sketched at the end of Chapter 1.

A developmental conception of human being as being-in-the-world could also put an end to, once and for all, the unfortunate legacy of pseudo-Promethean rhetoric that still defines existential philosophy for many people. And since the kind of development that is in question here is essentially bound up with the role of other people in our lives, it could be the occasion for an acknowledgment of a dimension of our lives that neither Heidegger nor Sartre, for all their differences, did justice to: our need for one another and for a cooperative mode of life that enables many more of us to realize our potentialities. We are currently committed to the idea of competition as the force by which social life is to be driven on the theory that it is only when people are set against one another that they will really give their best energies to undertakings that will eventually benefit everyone. The point I want to make is not that competition serves no purpose in the life of a society but rather that it must be in the service of cooperation at some deeper level.

Unhappily, it is at least doubtful whether that kind of subordination of the one to the other has ever been achieved and whether there has ever been a society in which, in one guise or another, domination has not been the underlying reality of the relationships among the human beings who compose it. Even so, there has also been a long-standing aspiration to change the terms of those relationships in a quite fundamental way and to show that the quality of life of both the powerful and the powerless under such arrangements is deficient in the extreme.

It is this aspiration that expresses itself in a willingness to go first in the circumstances that were described above and that offer so little in the way of any assurance of meaningful reciprocation. Anyone who has any experience of a life in which people are drawn together by bonds of esteem and affection has a stake in the strengthening of the system of mutuality that makes such relationships possible. It is true that there are circumstances in which the loss he might sustain if the actions inspired by this motive were not reciprocated has to be taken into account, if only because the interests of others are bound up with his own. But to borrow a phrase from Bernard Williams, something like a "moral incapacity" comes into play here once a profound identification of the self with its fellow human beings – that is, with its *Mitsein* – has been realized. It is not as though such a person could simply shift comfortably into a lower moral gear out of recognition of the force majeure of an adverse social environment. Whatever the hazards of persisting in such an attitude, they cannot seem worse to him than does the prospect of the general eclipse of that kind of mutuality. For such a person the good will be whatever strengthens the bonds of partnership by which people are united; and a distinction between self-interest and the general well-being will simply not be at all plausible.[15]

All of this is in marked contrast to the more common view that denies any special position to those who do not feel, as so many evidently do, that what is given to someone else is thereby denied to oneself. In this way of looking at things, the rational justification for such beneficent actions can only be that they satisfy a desire of those persons who perform them and thus constitute an element in their self-interest and the good it defines. The status of the good generated out of such motives will be viewed as an incidental bonus that enlarges the well-being that the practices that are ethically required are designed to bring about. In this way, the sovereignty of each "self" over the definition of its own interests remains unbreached and ethics will have to be understood as a set of common policies that promise to satisfy everyone's interests better than any other such set can.

Some such view as this finds expression in the currently popular conception of "values" that reduces a willingness to go first to the status of just such

---

15 In our own time one thinks of such figures as Dietrich Bonhoeffer and Simone Weil.

a value of a given individual and thus of his particular self-interest. To this, there is appended the further stipulation that there can be no guarantee that these values either would or should be shared. In other words, when someone who does not happen to cherish this particular value claims that he is happy, that claim has to be accepted as self-authenticating. There can, therefore, be no justification for assigning a special status to the attitude that makes our relations with others central to the possibility of happiness.

This ready compliance with the logic of that slippery term, "values," needs to be subjected to closer scrutiny. Although it is in universal use, and a concern for values is often regarded as being the touchstone of difference between those who take ethics seriously and those who do not, it really does not mean anything more than that what is so described is something that the person who so describes it likes or possibly likes very much, at least at that moment. This is shown by the fact that "values" are regularly referred to as being "mine" or "yours" and can be replaced and revised *ad libitum* as they could hardly be if their status were grounded in something deeper than our own preferences. It follows that if one chooses to apply the term to our relations with one another, these will turn out to be the creatures of these preferences in just the same way as our taste in colors or flavors is. "Values" cannot bind people to one another any more than the consumer preferences reflected in their shopping lists can.

In the argument I have been making here, it would not make any sense to use the term "value" to describe the sort of case in which someone goes first at the behest of ethical considerations but in circumstances in which the prospect of reciprocation is remote. The reason is quite simply that even if we were to adopt a usage that equates the good with "value" as that notion is currently understood, it would follow that the good represented by such an action would always be mine or yours or someone else's. But the good I have described is governed by the quite different logic of reciprocity that withdraws whatever it might be used to describe from the domain of anyone's exclusive proprietary control. Similarly, the notion of self-interest could hardly be applied to an action of this kind, not only because the likelihood of any advantage accruing to its author is so poor, but because the notion of interest itself has undergone a sea change. The interest – the good – of the author of this action is now understood to be bound up with that of its beneficiary in a way that makes any attempt to disentangle the one from the other futile, however plausible it may seem when the consequences of trying, say, to help a Jew in Nazi Germany are foreseeably immediate and severe. In general, the use of the language of values to render what can only be understood in terms of the relationships between one human being and another can only distort what is really involved, because it passes over this essential difference between the one and the other as though it were of no consequence.

It seems to me that we are now in a position to understand the connection between *Mitsein* and *Fürsorge* – our being, as Heidegger put it, "for the sake of others." There is, first of all, a strong sense that can be given to the latter notion and another that is certainly not weak but is in a clear sense less demanding. In this second sense, we can be said to be "for the sake of others" just by virtue of our acknowledgment of them as our partners in a form of life that is ethical in character. This means that we are bound to them by understandings that entail all kinds of mutual services that we are to render one another. In this sense we are all "for the sake of one another." But since the ethical character of this common life of ours is always more or less unstable and can on occasion be negated in really terrible ways, we may find ourselves in situations in which being for the sake of others takes on a new and very demanding meaning. Those are the occasions on which it is up to us whether we will honor the ethical requirements of our *Mitsein*, as for example in our relation to people who are being treated as not really human by others who are or may be in a position to make us pay dearly if we do not do likewise. Being for the sake of others in this situation means trying, under conditions of great risk, to keep alive a form of life that can survive, if it can, only if more people are able and willing to take that risk.

Moralists sometimes classify situations like this under the rubric of supererogation. This makes it seems that in ethics, as in other fields of human activity, there are overachievers – people who simply do more than is or can be required of them. If its intention is to honor such persons, this usage is unobjectionable; but it does seem to bypass the kind of point I have been making here. It divides people into the stars of the ethical life and the much humbler players; and it manages to suggest that the overachieving of the stars is simply an expression of a natural virtuosity. What this picture does not explain is what the motive (or need) could be for something as gratuitous as supererogation is apparently supposed to be. In the background, there seems to me to be a conception of a kind of ethical normality – everyone doing his or her allotted task in a well-designed system of rights and duties – that implicitly rejects the view put forward in the first section of this chapter. On that view, the ethical life is always in crisis and never secure or "normal"; and therefore there is always a pressing need to strengthen it in any way we can, even when our own interests may suffer.

CONCLUSION

I can imagine a number of reactions to the theses of this book, among them
one that might go something like this: "All this is fine and at times your evo-
cation of *Mitsein* even achieves a certain existential pathos. But you can
hardly deny that it is *vox humana* all the way and that, as a result, your account remains hopelessly confined to the very life that most needs to be informed by an order of truth transcending anything to which your kind of
analysis can give access. Wouldn't it be better if you simply acknowledged
that fact and made common cause with the relativists and the nihilists who
at least have the merit of not pretending they have anything better to offer?"

Another, quite different reaction might take the following line: "Why do
you think a 'ground of ethics' is needed at all? Such a ground would have
to be something absolute and utterly remote from the only kind of experience we have any familiarity with. As such, its status would be dubious at best
and that dubiety would have to be compensated for by the kind of dogmatic
rigidity that has always characterized such claims. Besides, people do not live
by the kind of understanding of themselves and others that you credit them
with. They live by custom and habit and by images of authority that are lo-
cal and particularistic in character. Perhaps you intend the claim to universal validity you make in some sense that would distinguish it from traditional
conceptions of moral truth; but it is very doubtful whether there is a real difference here. Wouldn't it be best if you simply aligned yourself with the people who hanker after absolutes in the field of conduct and gave up this pretense of a *via media?*"

Both these responses center on the idea of a ground of ethics; and they express dissatisfaction with my account of it. In the one case, this is because I don't go far enough in the direction of a conception of moral truth, and in the other because I come too close to it. But in the midst of this radical disagreement there is a paradoxical consensus. Both sides assume that anything that deserves to be called a "ground of ethics" at all must be the sort of thing that presents us with substantive principles of conduct from which the rest of our ethical code can be deduced. Since my version of such a ground does not do that, it is thought to be an untenable halfway house by both parties.

The convergence of these otherwise utterly different positions on this view of what a ground of ethics must be like simplifies my task in replying to them. What I would say to both is that their conception of an ultimate authority for ethical principles needs to be revised. They assume what I would call an external view of ethical authority – either to espouse or to reject it – that makes its source something wholly distinct from human beings and from human life; and yet it is from this wholly distinct something that the authority of ethical principles is supposed to accrue to them.[1] This is a picture that has obvious affinities with Platonic and Christian ideas and also with the view I called "objectivism" in the Introduction. Its effect is to disqualify as inadequate for these purposes everything that does not derive from a truth that is universal and timeless. For those who take this view, anything that is not "objective" in this super-strong sense of that term must be merely "subjective"; as such, it cannot establish what is uniquely right and wrong in the real world. For the other side as well, "objective" as applied to principles of conduct must entail that ethical assertions are true or false in some fairly straightforward sense. If someone claims, as I have done, that there is a ground *in re* for ethical distinctions, this must either be tantamount to a defense of moral truth or it cannot amount to anything much. In any case, any sponsor of such a view who seeks to evade this consequence must be deeply confused.

The trouble here lies in a failure to understand, first, that I am not postulating an idea of moral truth but rather a relationship among human beings that is preeminently realized in our capacity to acknowledge a common truth. Second, the role that we ourselves and our fellows play in this conception does not mean that what I am proposing must be some form of subjectivism. What keeps it from being "subjective" is the same thing that keeps it from being "objective" in the hopeless sense of a moral signpost that we come upon in the world. It is the fact that other human beings are acknowledged as being in principle as qualified as we ourselves are to choose

---

1 A famous example of this attitude is the statement in Ludwig Wittgenstein's *Tractatus Logico-Philosophicus* (London: Routledge and Kegan Paul, 1952), p. 183, that value must "lie outside the world." It may be, of course, that this idea has more to do with the way Wittgenstein conceived the world itself – as "everything that is the case" – than it does with anything else.

the guidelines under which we are all to live. If we could just stop thinking in terms that postulate some vaguely conceived "beyond" as the sort of thing that a ground has to be, we might see that the resources for an authentication of our principles of conduct are already available to us. Instead of living in a world in which "is" and "ought" are as dislocated from one another as they are in the well-known Humean story, our life with other like beings constitutes a relation between us that has a normative character, and it is that relation that finds expression in the "ought." It is, surely, the assumption that this world of ours is empty of such relationships and the normative consequences they generate that has led to the idea that these can come into it only by some sort of transfusion from another level of reality. So deep-seated is this conviction that there has been an almost complete failure to see that, to the extent that this language is appropriate at all, we ourselves, as the kind of entities we are, already are at that level. Unhappily, this is a fact that is more or less systematically obscured by the application to ourselves and to our lives of an ontology that is designed to deal with the entities we encounter in the natural world.

This is where the distinction that Heidegger proposes between entities (*Seiendes*) and their being (*Sein*) can be of great assistance to us. This is a distinction that replaces the dualistic objective/subjective contrast with a quite different ontological scheme that is much closer to the understanding of ourselves that dualism distorts out of all recognition. By "being" in this contrast, Heidegger means the presence of the entities that are in our world; and this presence is necessarily their presence *to* the kind of entity that eksists in the sense that it transcends its own spatiotemporal envelope and can thus be said not only to be in but to *have* a world. That kind of entity is *Dasein* – the There or locus of being as presence – and there are as many such entities as there are human beings. Human beings, so understood, can still be called subjects; but this does not mean that they live their lives under the sign of subjectivity as we ordinarily understand it. They are rather the entities that are the bearers of the being, in its several modalities of presence, of the natural world and of the historical and social world as well. Indeed, the only form of transcendence with which we have any real familiarity is that implicit in this presence and in our own temporality as the pastness and futurity of our world to which it gives us access.

Although Heidegger developed the concept of *Mitsein,* neither that concept nor its ethical implications can be said to have been at the center of his thought about being as such.[2] Instead, his primary concern was with the

---

2 It does not seem to have occurred to Heidegger (or at any rate not in a way that would have led him to elaborate this thought) that the chief significance of his conception of being as presence lay in what it implies about our relations with one another. The idea that reciprocal presence involves a kind of recognition that is implicitly ethical is simply not to be found in his work; and this is what the quotation at the beginning of the Introduction shows very

eclipse of being as presence – the way in which it becomes invisible and un-available to the very human beings whose lives are so closely bound up with it.[3] As a result he gave relatively little attention, beyond the account of *Mit-sein* in *Being and Time,* to being as the milieu in which we humans are with one another. That was unfortunate since it tended to minimize the role of being as the founding condition of the possibility of a world in which many ek-sistent beings can acknowledge one another within the framework of a relationship based on a common truth. Nevertheless, all the essential ele-ments for a constructive theory of such a world are available in Heidegger's ontology; and if we think of ourselves in terms of this picture, it is plain that the place of ethics is the locus in the world of the encounter with one an-other of entities of this kind.

These reflections suggest that Heidegger's thought might have developed in a different way that would have maintained a more readily recognizable affinity with the theses of *Being and Time* and, most especially, with the con-cept of *Mitsein.* It may be recalled that one of Heidegger's appellations for being is *to koinon* – that which is common. While that might be taken to mean what is common in the sense of a universal that can be instantiated by many particulars and is thus common to them all, it is unlikely that Heidegger would have construed it in such a Platonic way. For him, every *Dasein* has to be, as one might put it, "plugged" into being; and it is by virtue of being as presence that entities are present to a *Dasein* and one *Dasein* to another. What is common in *this* sense is plainly a milieu of presence; it is what is com-

clearly. "Ethics" is there conceived as a response to *Anwesenheit* (presence) and so to the fact of being as such, but not to one's fellow human beings who also "dwell" in the world as a do-main of truth. On this point, see C. F. Gethmann, "Heideggers Konzeption des Handelns in Sein und Zeit," in A. Gethmann-Siefert and O. Pogeller, eds., *Heidegger und die praktische Philosophie* (Frankfurt am Main: Suhrkamp, 1988).

3 It has been said that the theme of Heidegger's early writings was the meaning of being and that of the later ones, the truth of being. In other words, in the later works he was trying to deal with the fact that in the history of human thought, being as presence had never been properly recognized or acknowledged and had in fact been misconceived in a variety of ways. This history of obliviousness and misunderstanding was declared by Heidegger to be the his-tory of being itself rather than of human thought. Nevertheless, the distinction of human being lay, he claimed, in the fact that it was the scene on which being had manifested itself in its multiple disguises. Even so, it is hard not to feel that, if carried to its ultimate extreme, this attribution of everything important to the history of being would mean that the agency (and the responsibility) of human beings would be pretty much eliminated. In that case, the only stance for us would be what Heidegger calls *Gelassenheit* – a kind of quietistic "letting things be" and an avoidance of the strenuous self-importance to which, he evidently thinks, human beings are especially liable as long as they believe they can actually do something. The inevitable question this raises is whether *Gelassenheit* itself does not pose an option for us, and if it does, why this option should be the only one that is worth taking seriously. It does seem plausible, as Hannah Arendt has suggested, that this quietism represents an overreac-tion on Heidegger's part to the ghastly failure of his one great attempt to enter the world of action.

mon to us all. If Heidegger had taken more seriously this aspect of being as *to koinon*, that would have been tantamount to making a larger place for *Mitsein* in his account of being as such. In a way, this book has been an attempt to show what that line of development might have been.

When Heidegger's thought is reconstructed along the lines I have been suggesting, its relevance to our own intellectual and moral situation becomes a great deal clearer. For one thing, when ethics is understood in terms of an ontology based on the concepts of being and truth, our understanding of the status of ethics itself stands to benefit quite notably. More specifically, it will no longer have to justify itself in terms that presuppose the objective/subjective dichotomy. That distinction may be said to dominate our current science-based theories of the world; and it is typically used to demote ethics and indeed almost everything that is characteristically human to the not exactly honorific status of the subjective. Against this, I have been trying to show that the relationship between Ego and Alter (and thus the identity and difference of the one with and from the other) is neither subjective nor objective as these terms are usually understood, but is nevertheless as much a "fact" as anything could be. As such, it sets up the framework within which questions about the conduct of Ego and Alter vis-à-vis one another have to be understood. But if that is the case, then the whole conception of the ethical as something either subjective or objective – either *in* here or *out* there – is shown to be beside the point. Both these unappetizing alternatives can then be seen to be mutilated versions of a unitary context constituted by our own *Mitsein,* which it does not make sense to describe as being either the one or the other. This is to say that its status and that of our own lives as conceived in terms of ek-sistence and the being-with-one-another of ek-sistent beings elude classification under either of the alternatives that our current world picture makes available.

This does not mean that the notion of an eclipse of being would have had no place in Heidegger's thought. Everything Heidegger says about the elusiveness of being conceived as presence and its underivability from anything else is true; but it does not need to be expressed in terms of being's hiding itself – a notion to which I am unable to attach any determinate meaning. A different kind of explanation can be given for this elusiveness that would be modeled on what Heidegger says in *Being and Time* about the difficulty *Dasein* has in understanding itself otherwise than by a false assimilation of itself to inappropriate models drawn from entities in its world. In the case of being, it would be our inability to conceive it otherwise than in terms of entities (*Seiendes*). To this it may be added that if being were identified as a milieu of reciprocal recognition and thus of ethics, it would still be just as important as Heidegger thinks it is, not to confuse what it is – a domain of truth – with various surrogates like the Will to Power; and the only way to avoid this is to work out a concept of being as presence that can identify the false assimilation to which we are prone. Only if being is properly understood as a milieu of presence will the place of ethics be properly understood as the locus in the world of the encounter with one another of entities that ek-sist.

There is another point to be made here that may help to set this whole issue of subjectivity/objectivity in a different perspective. What I have in mind is simply the fact that there *are* such entities as we humans are – entities that can recognize one another as bearers of truth and relate to one another in a manner that in one way or another presupposes this fact. Now, we have been told again and again that we are not living at the center of a Ptolemaic universe and that it is only human vanity that keeps us from coming face to face with our largely accidental status within cosmic evolution. Still, it does appear that the official scientific account we have of that process hardly does justice to the fact that it is in our puny and in many respects rather wretched species that the truth of being is (or can be) realized. Doubtless, this silence on the part of scientists should not surprise us, given the limitations that the scientific world-view imposes on the kinds of facts it admits to its inquiries. But for anyone who is not constrained by these ground rules, it is hard to see how such a development as the one our own ek-sistence represents could be without some significance for a wider understanding of the reality in which our lives are embedded.

If the scientific community fails to enlighten us on this subject, the philosophers have at least tried. I think especially of one grandiose attempt that was made to give an account of that reality in terms that are halfway adequate to such facts as those of being as presence and *Mitsein*. Although Hegel no doubt demands more of his logic of being and nonbeing than any logic can hope to accomplish, two theses of the greatest importance do emerge from his thought. One of these is that the attempt to understand human nature in psychological terms and thus in effective isolation from its world and the being of that world is doomed to failure. The other is that the nature of these same human beings that in some sense *are* their world is, in a quite fundamental way, social. That social nature is what Heidegger has captured, in his very different philosophical idiom, in the concept of *Mitsein*.[4] What I have been trying to show is that the relationship that being as

4 In his book *De l'esprit: Heidegger et la question* (Paris: Editions Galilée, 1987), Jacques Derrida has pointed out that the term *Geist*, which Hegel used to convey the social character of human thought, begins to appear more frequently in Heidegger's writings during his Nazi period. The implication seems to be that this fact has some bearing on Heidegger's adherence to the Nazi cause and that, as a result, Heidegger's philosophy itself is somehow implicated in a sympathy for illiberal political movements. As it stands, this suggestion seems pretty farfetched. There are at least two questions Derrida would have to deal with before this charge could become even minimally plausible. Does the notion of *Geist* have anything like a central position in Heidegger's thought? And if it does, is there anything in the concept of *Dasein* that makes it necessary to construe the *Geist* under which it is subsumed in a manner that

presence mediates between entities that are familiar with it is ethical in a quite strong sense. To associate ethics with being in this way seems to me to meet the criteria for a nonsubjectivistic ethic in a manner that can hardly be improved on.

Nevertheless, it is a manner that is not familiar to us and will therefore meet with a good deal of resistance. We have become accustomed to the belief that our situation and prospects are best delineated by the scientific students of cosmic and biological evolution who press their inquiries outward from our own lives to the far reaches of space and time; and this appeals to our sense that we are pretty small potatoes in this whole process. It is a pity that, whatever they may discover, it will not include the history of being as presence if only because their conceptual vocabulary makes no place for it. It eludes their notice because, instead of being the kind of thing one can come upon in the world at large, it is something that has to be in place already if scientific inquiry as well as every other distinctively human function is to be possible. But if this book has established anything, it is that what is so presupposed has a plural and social character – that of *Mitsein*. Indeed, it would hardly be too much to say that if it is being – the being of entities – rather than entities as such in some kind of problematic abstraction from their being, that we are considering, being itself proves to be intimately bound up with *Mitsein*.

The great obstacle in the way of our really coming to terms with any of these matters is the almost universal conviction that we are living in a world about which only the natural sciences can make authoritative pronouncements. But since, as just noted, these sciences are precluded, by the logic of the kind of inquiry in which they engage as well as by their pride in what has been achieved by these methods, from making a place for either being as presence or ek-sistence in their theory of the world, there is a real sense in which we may be said to be oblivious of both and to live in a state of *Seinsvergessenheit* (forgetfulness of being), as Heidegger so often said. What is missing from Heidegger's own account, however, is any adequate acknowledgment of the implications of the kind of reciprocal presence that the plural nature of our ek-sistence entails. It is almost as though, in his own language, this aspect of his great theme had been "dimmed down" (*abgeblendet*) to a degree that made it effectively invisible to him. But if that is indeed the case, one feels there must be a deep connection between that obscuration of the ethical link with his fellow men and his tragic failure to understand what was happening around him in the Nazi period.

It might be tempting at this point to try to develop these observations

excludes the possibility of a free and critical contribution by individuals to the political life of a society? I am convinced that the answer to both these questions must be negative. What is true is that Heidegger's one attempt to formulate a social philosophy was not only a disastrous failure but betrayed the best inspiration of his own thought as well.

about the social character of being as presence somewhat further and to explore their affinities with religious ideas of the love of one's neighbor and the love of God. Even so, I do not think such speculations would be very promising, since whatever affinities there may be between these conceptions are more than balanced by formidable disaffinities that I see no way of setting aside. To this it might be added that the radical finitude of our condition precludes any possibility of insight into matters having to do with the nature and extent of a cosmic society of which our own *Mitsein* might be only a quite primitive affiliate. (Needless to say, questions about the presidency of such a society are also at best premature.) This is an area in which faith and hope doubtless have a place; but a doctrine about such matters seems hardly feasible under present circumstances.

What one can say is that Heidegger's vision of our age as a time of *Seinsvergessenheit* defines a crisis in the life of humanity that must be of the deepest concern to both religion and philosophy. Indeed, it would hardly be an exaggeration to say that a drama is being enacted in our lives in which everything that we have thought of as being precious to us is at stake, including our own ethical relationships to one another. It is at stake because all these things finally depend upon some at least partial understanding of what we are; and that understanding has been expressed during most of human history in a mythical form that is very vulnerable to the forces of *soi-disant* enlightenment. These have advanced under the banner of the scientific worldview, and they have now realized an almost complete "disenchantment" of the world. But in the debris left behind by this remarkable event is the language in which the understanding most people have had of their own lives and of their ties to others found expression.

In this situation the great religious traditions to which so many still look for guidance in a time of crisis appear to be almost helpless to deal with the challenge they face. They alternate between strategies of accommodation and rejectionism that never really address the painful dilemma in which they are caught. Philosophy, in a new, rather one-sided alliance with science, has for the most part chosen to remain above the battle by denying that there is any crisis worthy of its notice. But it is simply not possible for the ideal of a humanity that is more than the servant of its technologies to maintain itself in a world in which no one speaks for it. The reason no one speaks is that no one can; and the reason for that is that there is no acknowledged basis for the kind of self-understanding on the part of humanity that would be commensurate with this crisis.

It seems to me that this is where Heidegger's thought comes in, although it has been so compromised in the eyes of most people by his personal failings that it may never get a real hearing. Alone among the philosophies of our time, it has developed the conceptual resources and the historical understanding that can enable us to take the measure of our situation. That is a situation in which our blindness to being as presence makes it impossible to give any account of ourselves that is not artificially constrained by the need to shut out whole ranges of fact or to grant them recognition only as reconstrued in a manner that is putatively consistent with our commitment to the scientific world-view. Although Heidegger did not have much, if anything, to say about the specifically ethical aspects of this crisis, it is there, surely, that the damage is most evident, as is the general decline of the imaginative power and humane literacy that nourish the ethical life and that we do so little to form or to encourage.

It may be that, as Heidegger himself appears to have thought, we cannot by our own efforts overcome this extraordinary occlusion of our lives and our world. Even so, he seems to have envisaged a new beginning that would mark the end of the regime of reification under which we now live.[5] What is clear is that we can at least conceive, though in a very fragmentary way, an alternative to the present dispensation, and that out of that intimation of the possibility of "another beginning" we can try to speak another language in which the fact of being as presence and of our being with one another would be acknowledged, and not just in the learned jargon of a foreign language. Our effort must be to keep the world we live in from closing on itself, as it seems more and more to be in the process of doing, and in that way to prevent a total eclipse of being as presence and with it of a common life that is recognizably ethical.

5 In the *Gesamtausgabe* of Heidegger's works a volume appeared in 1989 under the title *Beiträge zur Philosophie: Vom Ereignis;* this book consists of *pensées* that were set down in the mid-1930s but not published. The central theme is the relation between *Dasein* (human existence) and *Sein* (being); the stages are traced in the progress of a form of thought that undertakes to move toward a "new beginning" and thus toward a mode of life in which the primacy of being as such in human life would be fully acknowledged.

INDEX